The Salvation of Maven Storm

The Salvation of Maven Storm

Finding the Love Relationship for
Which You Are Intended

Rick Krietemeyer

Foreword by Travis Penn

RESOURCE *Publications* · Eugene, Oregon

THE SALVATION OF MAVEN STORM
Finding the Love Relationship for Which You Are Intended

Resource Publications
An Imprint of Wipf and Stock Publishers
199 W. 8th Ave., Suite 3
Eugene, OR 97401

www.wipfandstock.com

PAPERBACK ISBN: 978-1-6667-0060-2
HARDCOVER ISBN: 978-1-6667-0061-9
EBOOK ISBN: 978-1-6667-0062-6

03/24/21

All Scripture quotations, unless otherwise indicated, are taken from the Holy Bible: New International Version. NIV © Zondervan

Contents

Foreword

HOT POCKETS, ELECTRIC GUITARS, and BetaMax video tapes. These things were all introduced to me by the man who wrote this book. So in some ways it seems strange that he has asked me to introduce this book to you.

Rick and I were very good friends from a young age. We went to the same Free Will Baptist church in Decatur, Illinois, and were influenced by many of the same wonderful people. Sunday afternoons were often spent at Rick's house playing music or throwing a football, and we always had lots of snacks thanks to his mom, Velma. She was also a great influence on me, but maybe we'll save that for the next book! We spent almost two full summers playing tennis in the evenings and ping-pong in my parents' basement during the day. We loved to challenge our church youth leaders, and we loved to prod and poke the friends in our youth group. Rick bugged one girl so much that she eventually married him! These days were good days and I'm so thankful for those times.

Rick went on to become a pilot and I went to college and then seminary and ended up in a small church in Salem, Illinois. It was not long after that Rick and Bev moved to Salem as well. They were a huge encouragement to our church, with Rick teaching young adults and Bev helping with Vacation Bible School and ministering to children. We knew how much they wanted children of their own, so when Emily came into their lives we were thrilled. It was hard to see them move away, but we knew the Lord had good things in store for them.

In those early days in Decatur, Rick improved my tennis game and my musical abilities and always pushed me to be a better person and a stronger Christian. From early on I realized that he wasn't someone who just talked about the Scriptures and about church, but he was trying to live them out. He taught me about treating people right. I've been around a lot of people who try hard not to speak gossip, but Rick is one of the few people that I've known who would do their best to even refuse to hear it. He has always challenged me to live out the truth that I knew in my heart.

When he asked me to review his book, I immediately was brought back to how clearly Rick can communicate. In almost every chapter of this book there are fantastic illustrations that take sometimes difficult or abstract ideas and make them easy to understand. For anyone who is wanting to grow in their walk with their Lord, or help a new believer get off to a good start, I think they will find a lot of encouragement in the pages to follow.

We live in a time where the American church appears to be weakening and the gospel is often watered down. We need to rekindle a fire among our people that removes our apathy and pushes us back to diligence as we labor for the Savior who gave his all for us.

There can sometimes be confusion about what being a Christian is all about. While church attendance and Bible reading plans are good disciplines, this life we are to live is not about trying to be a good person. It is about a loving relationship between us and our Creator. It's not just us receiving his gracious gifts, but living to please the one who loves us beyond measure. Throughout this book I think you'll be reminded again and again just how much God loves you and is chasing you down to have a relationship with you. Rick's analogies bring a fresh perspective to timeless truths and he'll have you thinking about your relationship with God all over again.

Thank you for your friendship, Rick, and thank you for encouraging God's church with this book.

Travis Penn
Pastor, CrossLife Free Will Baptist Church,
Indianapolis, Indiana

Acknowledgments

To ALL OF THE people who helped me with this book. The cover may show one author but it could not have been done without other people.

To the members of my book club, specifically Dorthy Harris, Robyn House, and Linda Smith. Writing this book began with their encouragement. I would write a chapter and have them review it. You could say they were the first ones to criticize my work. They, along with the Clear Springs Free Will Baptist Church members, are the people I rely on to help me get through life. Thank you for being there for me.

To Pastor Jim Harris. We have spent the last ten years discussing theology and I have learned much from him. He and his wife, Kim, have been a support to my family and I am happy to have found such a caring pastor.

To Pastor Travis Penn. Travis has been a friend I know I can trust, no matter the circumstances of my life. He helped me keep the theology of this book from going astray. He has helped me in many ways, including my walk with Jesus. I have learned much from him. It would be hard to find better people than Travis and his wife, Wendy, whom I am proud to call friends.

To my daughter, Emily. Emily and I are very different people but she keeps me honest. She is not afraid to call me out when I need to be called out. The way her mind works makes me think deeper than I normally would. Being her father has been one of the best experiences of my life, and our relationship has helped me understand and strengthen my relationship with Jesus.

To my wife, Bev. She continues to amaze me. If I want to see what a Christian looks like, I need look no further than Bev. I wish I were able to see things the way she sees them. Her love and encouragement keep me going. Being in a covenant relationship with her for over twenty-five years has taught me what a good relationship looks like, and it has helped me with my walk with God.

Introduction

THERE ARE FOUR BASIC levels of learning.[1] The first level is *rote*. Rote is where you hear something and are able to mimic it back without understanding. Do you remember the first time you heard $A^2 + B^2 = C^2$? I heard it in sophomore geometry class. They make it easy to memorize, but that does not mean I understood the meaning.

They call it the Pythagorean Theorem. Once introduced, our teacher then began the process of explaining. If you know the length of two of the sides of a right triangle, you can compute the third with C being the hypotenuse. After a short time, I understood the theorem. *Understanding* is the second level of learning.

Then the teacher wanted us to apply our understanding and assigned us a bunch of homework problems. *Application* is the third level of learning and it reinforces our understanding. After applying this new knowledge many times on sheets of paper, I had it down pretty well.

So what? Have you ever heard somebody say "I will never use this useless math"? I learned it, but it does no good unless you are able to find a way to use it in a real-life situation.

Then one day, years later, I was talking to a friend who was helping his friend. They were trying to find a way of putting a crude baseball field on the back of their property. How would they put the bases out without making it all crooked? They were starting with home plate. The distance between each base is ninety feet. They would measure from home to first, then first to second, then second to third. The problem was that they never had exactly ninety feet from third to home. Why? The angles between those other bases were not exactly ninety degrees. The lengths can only be equal if it is a perfect square.

1. *Aviation Instructor's Handbook*, 3–14

Somebody had an idea to start with putting home base down first and second base down second. Then they could make first and third bases equal distance. That was a good idea. For that, we would need to know how far it was from home to second base. This was a time in history where we did not have the internet to look up that answer. Guess what? I knew how to figure that out. Knowing the bases form a perfect square I could cut the square into two right triangles. The distance from home to second base would be the hypotenuse. The distance on the other sides is a given ninety feet. Eureka! I was able to use my knowledge of the Pythagorean Theorem to solve a real-life issue. That level of learning is *correlation* and should be the level of learning we strive to reach in all fields we study.

As I have grown in my relationship with Jesus Christ, I noticed some correlations. These correlations came in the form of my relationship with my family, friends, and coworkers. How the family is set up is no mistake. God made Eve as a companion for Adam. They were told to have children. There are many verses in the Bible where we are told how to treat one another within the family environment. God made male and female as a complementary system. The female was to take on the role as wife and mother. There were certain responsibilities that went along with that role. The male was to take on the role as husband and father. There were certain responsibilities that went along with that role.

The Lord set it up this way for a reason. This family environment is an image of our life with God. When we join into a covenant with another, whether that be marriage to a spouse or salvation to Christ, we enter a love relationship unlike any other. We need to look no further than our own lives to see God's desire.

As the husband is the head of the wife, Christ is the head of the church.[2] How much is the husband supposed to love his wife? As much as Christ loves the church and gave himself up for her.[3] Children are to obey their parents in the Lord, as this is similar to how we are supposed to obey our Father in heaven. Similarly, parents are not supposed to exasperate their children, and God will not exasperate us either.[4]

When I first started down this path of Christianity, I did not fully understand. I am slow to learn, so it took time. I asked a lot of "why" questions.

2. Eph 5:23, NIV.

3. Eph 5:25.

4. Eph 6:4.

Why does God care if I covet? Why does God care if I get angry? Why would that bother him? Why does he give us commands like a dictator?

What I found was something different. Christianity is not about a bunch of rituals and orders we have to obey. I can see how some would think of it this way. Christianity is about a relationship. I did not fully understand this at first. My personal experiences helped me understand that better. With this book, I have provided some of those personal experiences, which you may be able to relate to, in an attempt to correlate those experiences to theological truths.

I have divided this book into three sections. I saw dating and marriage as very similar to how we come to God. I call the first section "The Single Life" and discuss the process of developing a love relationship. Having a relationship with God is very similar to having a relationship with a family.

I call the second section of the book "The Engaged Life" and discuss commands of God. I discuss the types of things God desires from us. Just as I found out what my wife wanted before we got married, there are things Jesus wants from us as we join into a covenant relationship. There are various commands God has given us to follow. I attempt to show why God gave us these commands. We want to make sure we understand what relationship we are getting into before we commit to it. You would not want to get married and then learn what your spouse expects of you, just to find out you were not compatible.

I call the last section of the book "The Married Life" and explore how great life is with Jesus. I see a correlation between the marriage ceremony to a spouse and accepting Jesus into our lives. I also discuss what our new married life will be like by seeing what he promises us in return.

I can state firsthand that being in a relationship with Jesus has made my life exponentially better. My prayer is that, through these words, you find that relationship also.

The Single Life

CHAPTER 1

A Betting Man

(Is Seeking God Worth the Gamble?)

I AM NOT A gambler. I have learned to accumulate over time instead of all at once. I like playing games, like poker, but we just pretend with some type of fake money. First, I am not good at gambling, so I know I would lose my money. Second, I do not really get the appeal. Sure, there is a chance I could get rich, but money should not be our goal in life. Money is a tool we use to accomplish the will of God and take care of our families and others. In other words, we use it to build our relationships. The love of money pulls us away from what is most important.[1] The most gambling I do is in the stock market, and then I am a long-term investor, concentrating on my retirement fund, which makes it less risky. As a pilot, I have been trained to eliminate risk or mitigate it when it cannot be avoided.

Some people enjoy the sport of gambling. It is estimated that hundreds of billions of dollars are spent on gambling every year.[2] There is something about gambling that appeals to some people. I have an acquaintance who goes to the casino almost every weekend. I am not sure if that means they have a gambling problem or not. Maybe I should be concerned.

The Super Bowl was just two weeks away. A friend of mine had been considering putting a wager on the big game. In preparation, he did an extensive amount of research. He wanted to know all of the statistics involved with both teams. He listened to experts in the field. He knew the odds and the spread. He spent an incredible amount of time and effort

---

1. 1 Tim 6:10.
2. Sherman, "Legal Gambling," para. 9.

in preparation for this bet. I am not sure the amount he was betting but I knew he was going to make the wager. Finally, it was time for the game and he placed his bet.

Now, my friend is usually a quiet person. I never see him getting anxious or excited. As the game progressed, his emotions were all over the place. At first, he was so mad because the team he bet on did terribly in the first half of the game, and they were going into the locker room with a big deficit. We always got along but he was not very pleasant to be around during half time. He was so focused on losing his money that he had trouble socializing properly. As the third and fourth quarters progressed, his mood changed. The team he picked to win actually came back to win. At the time, it was considered the biggest comeback in Super Bowl history. He was exuberant, jumping up and down, and celebrating because the team he chose won the game and he won the bet.

Why would a person put that much effort and emotion into one bet? He put that much effort into it because he understood that putting effort into finding information would lead to making a better decision. Making better decisions means taking less risk. He was emotional because he knew the possibility of losing money existed. He cared about his money, and who can blame him for that? He had worked hard to earn it. If he had gone into the wager without doing research, there was a better chance of losing.

Caring about something causes us to take action. Caring about something gets us excited. Caring about something causes us to prepare for the upcoming big game.

Right now, we are playing a game. It is a game we call life. (Not the board game.) Some of us are just babies and just beginning the game. Some of us are older and in the final quarter of the game. Is there a winner in this game? I do not see the winner as the person with the most stuff when they die. You cannot take it with you when you die, so what does it matter how much you accumulate? I see the winner as the one who gets the God relationship correct.

Is there really a place our souls go after we die? What if one of those places has the potential to be bad for all of eternity. If so, then why are we so apathetic toward it? Why do we care so little that we sit around doing nothing about it? Instead of doing research and learning, we sit around talking about the weather, the football game, the latest on social media, and politics. I am not saying those things are bad, but we never leave any room for what is important. Our downtime is filled with mind-numbing videos and soul-crushing social media. If the chance of such a place exists, then there should be nothing in this world as important as gaining knowledge about God and making sure we get it correct.

Even if I do not think such a place existed, it would be worth my time and effort to do the research. Research gives us information. Information gives us the power to make better decisions. Instead, so many of us are just happy to be lazy. It takes effort to use our brains. Therefore, we just go through life performing meaningless works and hope it works out in the end. We build castles in the sand thinking we are accomplishing greatness. Like the Greeks, we chase after intelligence, puffing up, and thinking of ourselves as great. The only thing that matters, and is worth chasing, is God and the things that go with that relationship. This worldly life is but a mist that appears for a little while and then vanishes.[3] Your soul is the thing that will last for all of eternity. Matthew 6:33 states, "But seek first his kingdom and his righteousness, and all these things will be given to you as well."[4] Seek First! Seek First! Seek First!

Blaise Pascal, a French mathematician, physicist, inventor, writer, and philosopher, came up with a different type of wager.[5] Pascal argued that every person on Earth places a wager. The bet is whether God exists or does not exist. Some bet God exists and live their life in a way they think is pleasing to him. Some bet God does not exist and live their life the way they desire. What is the wager? Instead of losing wealth, or any such temporary possessions, we bet our everlasting souls for all eternity.

Just like there is no way to be 100 percent certain which team will win the Super Bowl, there is no way to be 100 percent certain that God exists, just like there is no way to be 100 percent certain that God does not exist. It is anybody's game to win, or lose, until your personal clock gets to zero. Then you get to see the final score and see who wins the bet.

If God does not exist, then the loser is the one who bet on God's existence. In this situation, both betters receive the exact same afterlife reward when they die. They both lose consciousness forever, turn back into dust, and that is all there is to it. I guess you can call it a participation trophy. In this case, there is no such thing as a soul that lives forever. The biggest thing this person loses are finite pleasures or earthly luxuries because they are

---

3. Jas 4:14.

4. Matt 6:33.

5. Hajek, "Pascal's Wager," 2018.

seeking God during their lifetime instead of wealth or any other temporary goods that mean nothing once they die.

If God does exist, then the loser is the one who bet on God's non-existence. In this situation, the winner has the chance to receive infinite gains and the loser infinite losses. In this case, there is such a thing as a soul that will continue forever. It was for this reason Blaise Pascal thought a rational person should live their life seeking after God wholeheartedly. The endgame consequences were too big to ignore.

My friend cared about his money enough to do the research it took to have the advantage. He got excited about the possibility of losing it. Unfortunately, many people do not get excited about Pascal's wager. Not many people get excited about their souls. If we could fully understand how serious it is then maybe we could get more excited. If we care that much about money, which is not something we can take with us when we die, then why do we not care about our everlasting souls just as much, if not more? Do we not believe this is a possibility? Is our soul meaningless to us until we face death? Is it because we do not want to think about the possibility of going to hell forever? Do we think we are entitled and God will protect us no matter what we do on this Earth? With all that is at stake, how can we for a moment become apathetic toward eternity? We must not care that much about our souls.

I wonder if we think following God will mean giving up the things we want. We look at the things of this world and covet. The person who has nothing desires something. The person who has something desires more. We are not seeking God first, and we should be.

This reminds me of my high school days. I was a bit of a late bloomer. I did not have my first date until after I graduated. Do not get me wrong, I probably would have stammered through the word "yes" if asked out, but it was not a priority. If you wanted to get a hold of me, you could find me playing tennis, golf, ping-pong, billiards, basketball, etc. Playing sports was more fun to me at that time. I did not care to be in a relationship. I knew being in a relationship would take time away from those other things. I did not want to give up my wants. What I was not seeing was how great it was to be in a relationship, even if it meant giving up other things. I found out later, when I married my wife, just how great a relationship is.

Maybe you are like that today. You do not want to be in a relationship with Jesus because it will take too much of the things you want away. Maybe it will take too much of your time. Maybe you think it will just be too hard.

You want what you want and not what the relationship will demand. What you are not seeing is how much joy the relationship will provide. You do not see how much peace the relationship will provide. You still have to find the love for Jesus. This takes work. It takes study. It takes excitement. Once you take time to work and fall in love with Jesus, your attitude changes. Being in a relationship with Jesus is the only thing that matters. The rest of our lives fall into place when that relationship with Jesus is correct.

Just like that Super Bowl gamble, we have already made our bet, but it is slightly different with God. He is still working on us.[6] For those who have made the bet against him, he is patient, giving us a chance to do the research. Second Peter 3:9 states, "The Lord is not slow in keeping his promise, as some understand slowness. Instead he is patient with you, not wanting anyone to perish, but everyone to come to repentance." He is giving us a chance to gain the critical information we need to make an informed decision. Every hour we waste means we get closer to the end of the game without gaining critical information. His desire is that nobody miss out on the greatest experience ever. We are not stuck with our initial bet. He gives us time to change it if we wish. The gamblers have the chance to change their bet up until the clock gets to zero.

For those who have made the bet in favor of God's existence, we need to continue the research in an effort to gain critical information, which will strengthen our bet. We need any new information that will help us select the most logical choice. We need any new information to help others see the way. Never be afraid of the truth. We still have time to get others to change their choice, but we had better hurry because the clock keeps counting down.

We owe it to ourselves, our loved ones, and the human race to figure out if God exists and how we can prevent infinite losses, because we sure cannot avoid the bet. It cannot be that hard to perform some research and look for this God. Deuteronomy 4:29 states, "But if from there you seek the Lord your God, you will find him if you seek him with all your heart and with all your soul."[7] Put your busyness behind you. You have to seek with *all* your heart, not just a part of it. You have to seek with *all* your soul, not just a part of it. If you do not have room in your lives to do the research, then you will not find him. Luke 11:9–10 states, "So I say to you: Ask and it will be given to you; seek and you will find; knock and the door will be opened

6. Phil 1:6.

7. Deut 4:29.

to you. For everyone who asks receives; the one who seeks finds; and to the one who knocks, the door will be opened." Jesus promised this to us. He did not say he might give or might open the door. He guaranteed it. We must leave our bias and suppressed belief behind and honestly search.

There are those that do not want to follow Jesus. They want to continue doing things their way and it is just not worth their time and effort. This is due to greed. Greed is the very reason we seek something other than God. People want things their way.

Instead of searching personal desires, our hearts should pursue righteousness, godliness, faith, love, endurance, and gentleness.[8] In other words, we should seek the things Jesus told us to seek.

Is your everlasting soul worth the effort? To not seek God is foolish. To be apathetic about your future is laziness. To be uncaring means we will lack information. Lacking information is the safest way to lose the bet when the clock gets to zero and the final buzzer goes off.

8. 1 Tim 6:11.

CHAPTER 2

Complete Fulfillment

(Finding Meaning in a Big World)

EVENTUALLY WE START HAVING a desire to find somebody to love and for somebody to love us. It is just something that happens naturally. Once we find we want to search for that relationship, we have to take the next step. We have to go out on dates. Dating is hard! Some people are good at it. I was not. I was shy, introverted, and lacked self-esteem. I am not talking about taking my wife out to a movie or restaurant. I am talking about the time in my life when I was single and did not know whom I would be dating next. I hated the whole process of finding somebody, asking her out, and figuring out an event to attend. Then you had to play this game between telling them who you are but not being annoying. Do you hold their hand? Do you kiss them at the end of the night? It is not comfortable, and I like comfort.

Why would I put myself through such agony? It is because I had to go through that process to get at what I really desired. I desired to be in a committed relationship. A truth- and secret-telling, comforting, future planning, sacrificing, encouraging, loving, committed relationship. There is something within each of us that desires closeness. Closeness to a mate. Closeness to friends. Closeness to family. We long to have those relationships.

What brings about these feelings? I wondered if we are built with these characteristics for a reason. Therefore, I tried to answer one of the biggest questions ever attempted.

What is the purpose of life? It could not be that hard to come up with an answer, could it? It should not take too long to come up with that answer, should it? Actually, philosophers have been examining this question for thousands of years. Have you ever given it any thought? There have been many philosophers who gave their opinions on the purpose of life. Historical examples I have heard include: to explore and experience; to experience happiness; to become our greatest version; to prepare yourself for the next stage; to live in the present moment; to learn; to spread kindness and peace; to leave a legacy; and to cultivate your gifts. I am sure there are more.

One of the fundamental needs for humans is to understand our significance in life. We need to feel like we make a difference somewhere. We have this inward drive to feel important. Our purpose in life is why we get out of bed in the morning. Our purpose influences our behavior. Our purpose shapes our goals and offers a sense of direction. Without it, life would not seem important.

We need to start by making a distinction between purpose *of* life and purpose *in* life. When I say purpose *of* life, I mean why life exists in the first place. When I say purpose *in* life, I am stating that we already exist, and because of that existence, we need to find meaning in our life.

These terms are often used interchangeably. For instance, a philosopher might state the purpose of life is to be happy. This does not mean he or she is saying we exist to be happy. What is being said is that it does not matter how we came into existence but being happy in the moment is what is important. Being happy brings contentment and inner peace. Inner peace is what is important. This purpose does not answer what I call the "why" question. I consider this statement to be a purpose *in* life comment. Actually, the purpose *in* life is what most people are truly interested in finding, and that is what philosophers attempt to answer.

I think philosophers, as well as most people, are asking the wrong question. We can assign many goals to fill that need for a purpose *in* life. We could shove thousands of tasks and goals into that box. We might think of our jobs, children, nonprofits, hobbies, etc., but those reasons do not explain why and are not the reason we exist in the first place.

Does it even matter that we understand the purpose of our existence? I believe the only way we can truly find complete fulfillment with our given life is if we figure out our purpose for existence. We need to figure out the why question. Then we can make our purpose *in* life match to fulfill the purpose *of* life. When I understand why I am here, then it gives meaning, and what I do comes into focus.

Let me give you an example on a nonliving item. A screwdriver is created to put screws into wood and other materials. Now, I could use it as a paperweight and it would have meaning *in* existence, but I would not be using it for its intended purpose. It is not completely fulfilling its intended purpose *of* existence. As a living being, I have an intended purpose *of* life and I need to find it if I wish to be completely fulfilled. Then I can make my purpose *in* life match.

The question of existence really boils down to one of two camps. Do you view it as biological or intellectual? These are just the two terms I created for identification.

On the one hand, some believe the universe exploded from nothing without the aid of an intelligent being. In that theory, the universe is over fourteen billion years old and we have evolved into our current state without any outside help. This is what I call biological. Biological processes are the physical means by which I exist.

If we are truly here through some random process, then there really is no meaning behind our existence. Being brutally honest, my life would have no meaning at all. Donald A. Crosby said, "There is no justification for life. . . . Those who claim to find meaning in their lives are either dishonest or deluded. In either case, they fail to face up to the harsh reality of the human situations."[1] Mr. Crosby believed in the biological system as a means of existence and honestly faced the inevitable end of that truth.

King Solomon, whom some consider to be very wise, said, "Meaningless! Meaningless! Utterly meaningless! Everything is meaningless."[2] Can you feel the frustration in his words? He wrote this at the end of a very full life. That is because he tried to find meaning in all areas. When you read his work in Ecclesiastes, it comes across as a scientist who had attempted many experiments looking for meaning yet had come up empty. He had anything and everything a person could ever want, yet the temporary products this life produces left him empty.

We need to be honest and quit fooling ourselves. If we were just placed here by a random process then why do we continue to seek a purpose? It is because our inner being craves it. We need to have purpose *in* our lives or life would not be worth living.

People will search and search for understanding and meaning yet come up empty because they do not know the reason for their existence. They start by putting meaning into their school projects. Doing well makes them feel good and makes their parents proud. Then they usually try to put

1. Crosby, *Specter of the Absurd*, 30.

2. Eccl 1:1.

meaning into their work. Then their jobs do not go the way they planned and they are dissatisfied with that meaning. Then they put meaning into their marriages. Then they put meaning into their kids. Then they put meaning into their hobbies. They just keep searching. To satisfy their need, they reach out with different answers. These answers do provide meaning for them, like the screwdriver being a paperweight, but they all fall short of complete fulfillment.

The second camp to explain existence is what I call intellectual. When I think about my personal existence, there was more than just biological processes involved. My parents had to make a choice. Do we have a child or not? I exist because my parents wanted me here. An intelligent being had to decide my existence.

Many people have children. A harder question would be to answer the why question again. Why did my parents decide to procreate? Why does anybody choose to procreate? Reasons I have heard people give for having children include such items as to carry on the family name, to give another the chance to enjoy existence, to create something that is like them, social pressures, expectations, and many more. I am positive they truly believe these meanings, but children are a long-term investment, so let us take a long-term look.

Children are very expensive. In 2018, it was estimated that to raise one child from birth to age seventeen could cost over \$233,000.[3] In 2018, that would buy a very nice house, and it does not even include helping your child through the transition to adulthood independence like college. It is possible that parenthood could be killing us sooner due to sleep deprivation and worry. Were you hoping to die young? You will end up running them around to various activities like getting up at 5 a.m. on a Saturday for a tennis tournament, so having children means your leisure time is done. Did you not want to sleep in on Saturday? It has been shown that the world is becoming too crowded. Are you trying to contribute to the destruction of Earth? As they grow into teens, they will be angry with you, possibly going as far as to say they hate you. Did you really want to bring somebody into the world that would hate you? They will get into trouble. Sometimes super bad trouble, and you might get dragged into that process. There are numerous reasons that tell us having kids would be terrible for us.

The truth is, when you hold your baby for the first time, all of that other stuff leaves your thoughts. You are only thinking about how much

---

3. Fiorillo, "Cost to Raise a Child," para. 1.

love you have for that child. If we were to be brutally honest, love is the real reason we have children. If we were to view children as an investment, all of those negatives would put us so far in the hole, any of those other reasons would never bring the balance to the positive side. It would never be worth the investment. However, love is invaluable. Love is one of the fundamental needs we crave. We desire to have a close relationship with others. When all else is going bad, we can take comfort in a loving relationship. As much pain as we are going to be in, the love of a child turns the investment positive. My parents wanted a child to love.

What I have explained would be a purpose *of* my life, but why life at all? Is there an intelligent being that created the universe? If God does exist, he would have to be all-powerful, but he would not be able to go against his own character. Is there something God would not be able to do? Imagine for a moment that you are God. You created the entire universe out of nothing. You created the angels and designed them for specific purposes. What is it that you could possibly want, yet not get on your own? The only thing I can think of is love.

Can God create us and force us to love him? He can create us. He could force us to serve him. He could force us to tell him we love him repeatedly like a robot. That is not true love. There is only one way God can experience the type of love he desires. He has to give us free will. We have to have the ability to choose or deny. The same thing happens with our other relationships. We cannot force our kids to love us. We cannot force our dates to love us. We offer them the opportunity and leave it in their hands. We have to love freely or not at all.

I know I said I am not a gambling man, but there is no doubt that this is a gamble. Giving freely will not only mean a person can truly love you, it also means they can freely reject you. Just like a teenager telling their parent they hate them, the same thing happens to God. There is no doubt he wants to have a loving relationship with us, but he loves us too much to force us into a relationship with him. He wants us to love him freely. If we do not want that, he has to let us go. I hope you caught that, because it's important. He has to let us go.

Going back to Ecclesiastes, King Solomon recites twelve chapters of things that are meaningless and ends the book with these words. "Now all has been heard; here is the conclusion of the matter: Fear God and keep his commandments, for this is the duty of all mankind."[4] This is the only place Solomon found complete fulfillment.

First Corinthians 8:6 states, "Yet for us there is but one God, the Father, from whom all things came and for whom we live; and there is but one Lord, Jesus Christ, through whom all things came and through whom we live."[5] That verse alone tells us why we are here. We were created by God and for God. Man is designed for that relationship. I believe an intelligent being created us, in his image,[6] so that a loving relationship could exist between him and us. This is the only reason we have the same desires. He understands how much of a pain we are going to be, just as we understand how much of a pain our children are going to be. For the same reasons that we ignore those bad things and still have children, God still wants to have a relationship with us. We are created for that purpose.

Growing up I wanted to be an architect. Then I learned how much math was involved, so I gave it up. I used to be terrible at math. I changed my career to pilot. I had heard they made a lot of money. I can drive a car. How much harder could it be? I only thought about me and my desires. Those things will only satisfy for a brief time, and then they will leave us empty. At some point, most people become unhappy with their careers. By the time they figure it out, they are stuck. We stay in our careers because we do not want to lose money, our livelihoods, and our materialistic stuff. I call it the trap. I certainly felt empty. I tried different things, and grew in my career. I kept coming up empty. Once I realized my purpose *in* life was to have a relationship with God and others, I was then able to focus on complete fulfillment. I now search for what God wants me to do, and wherever I end up in my job, I feel much better. I may still work in aviation but my goal is to please God.

Without going into too much detail, in 2016 I was offered an opportunity to change my job. This opportunity meant a lot more money and the job was easier. I gave it some thought. The money kept me thinking yes. It is a powerful motivator. I have been around long enough to know money will not keep me happy. I took money out of the equation. I told myself, what if that job paid me the same amount I was getting now, and the decision became clear. I decided to stay in my current job. My coworkers thought I was crazy for not taking it. Why? Because it was more money. When you

4. Eccl 12:13.

5. 1 Cor 8:6.

6. Gen 1:27.

take power, money, and earthly stuff out of the equation, and just focus on how you can serve God, things become clearer and it is so much more satisfying and freeing.

Some keep reaching. They think if they could only have that one more thing, they could finally be happy. If they could reach that promotion, they could finally be happy. Do you ever stop to say to yourself, "If I can have Jesus, then I can finally be happy"?

We continue this search for the purpose *in* life because we fight against our existence. We might find meaning, like being a paperweight. We might find purpose *in* our lives through our jobs, children, or any other activity, but we exist to have a relationship with God. We will never reach complete fulfillment until we reach that committed relationship for which we are designed—a relationship with Jesus, the creator of the world.

CHAPTER 3

The Inclusive Country Club

(It Is Not about Being Good Enough)

I ALWAYS TELL PEOPLE I grew up poor. We did not have much growing up. My brother was older than I was so I got some of his stuff as I got older. I used to feel embarrassed about this. I played tennis in high school. There were times the coach would drop us off after a tournament and I hated it because it would mean my teammates seeing our house, which was in a poor neighborhood. Looking back, it all seems so silly because being rich or poor is not what matters. I now understand that being poor does not make me an inferior being. My value as a person is not held in the amount of money in my bank account. In my younger years, it actually had quite an effect on me. It was a part of the reason I lacked self-esteem.

As poor as I tell people I was, it was nothing compared to my father. My father grew up ridiculously poor. There were seven children and the only toy he could remember having was a little red wagon. They would take turns pulling each other around. They did not have many of the modern conveniences we enjoy today. They even had to take baths outside in a metal tub. The earliest he remembered working was at age ten. They had a bowling alley with three lanes, and when the bowlers would knock down the pins, he would roll the ball back to them and rearrange the pins accordingly. This was before automatic ball returns and pin-setting machines. He had odd jobs until he was sixteen. He felt his life was going nowhere and he had no future in that small, sleepy town, so he begged his parents to sign the paperwork so that he could go into the Marine Corps early. They did and off he went to Asia at seventeen years old. The Korean War had just ended and his time there was not too bad.

My father was one of the hardest workers I knew. Growing up the way he did ingrained in him a work ethic that everybody admired. On more than one occasion, I remember him saying, "A good day's wage for a good day's work." If you hired my father for a job, you knew the job would be done right and be complete by the end of the day.

I am sure it did not transfer over, but my father tried to instill this work ethic into my brother and me as we were growing up. I remember mowing lawns for money as young as ten years old. We were always looking for opportunities for jobs.

When I was fourteen years old I saw an ad in the paper for golf caddy wanted at the Country Club. You had to be at least fourteen years of age. The job consisted of carrying golf bags, helping golfers, replacing divots, etc.

We had a few public golf courses around town but this was the Country Club. This was an exclusive club. Not just anybody could join or play. In those days, a person could not just go sign up, pay their fee, and get on the course. First, they had to receive a recommendation from an existing club member. Then the club would vote based upon their social and economic status around town. Then they could join for a certain amount of money. When you are fourteen and think you might be working around such fanciness, it gets you excited.

At the time, I could only work on Saturdays. I would go in to work. They would assign me to a player. We would walk eighteen holes carrying their bags on our backs. We would run ahead of them spotting their ball and pointing it out. The first player on the green meant his caddy got the privilege of grabbing the pin. Walking eighteen holes would take about four hours to complete. For this great job, we earned a fantastic seven dollars. You read that right, seven dollars.

Granted this was 1982, but I hope current country clubs have changed their ways, because this was a terrible job. I remember getting yelled at by the boss once because I was a few feet behind my golfer, instead of ahead of him, as we walked down the fairway. We were supposed to walk ahead of them. The members were rich and powerful people around town. They did not treat the caddies well. Four hours of backbreaking, sweat inducing, demeaning work for a measly seven dollars. If you did a good job, you might have received a tip. You can call me a quitter but that job did not last long before I said enough. However, I did not quit before learning lessons that I could apply to my life and correlate with God.

Later in life, I was working an office job. We lived in a part of the country that was very much Christian. A coworker said they were moving because the people around them were not open-minded and it was driving them crazy. I could not help but wonder what he meant by that. He and his wife thought the neighbors were very closed-minded. He thought there was fundamental truth in all religions and Christians were not open to that kind of thinking. My coworker said that it seemed like not everybody around them was willing to consider other religions as a way to God. If you were not Christian then it felt like you were being ostracized. It was as if God was the head of the heavenly country club and Christians were the members excluding others around town.

Hey, this is something I can understand! I could relate as I have seen that before. The way that he was looking at it was that Christians were arrogant, thinking they had the only way to God. He saw life as climbing up the mountain to God. Each religion is a different path. Even though we are on different paths, all paths eventually lead to God. This is what he meant by being open. Those around them were not willing to think the same way. This bothered them so much they literally moved halfway across the country in the hopes of finding an area not so judgmental.

I told him I could see how Christianity might look like an exclusive country club, but let us take a closer look. First, let us not blame Christians. It is Christ himself who said in John 14:6, "I am the way, the truth, and the life: no man cometh unto the Father, but by me." He did not say he is *A* way, but *THE* way. He did not say he has *A* truth, but is *THE* truth. He did not say there are other ways to God. He said he is the *ONLY WAY*.

At first glance, it appears that Jesus is that person that keeps the town folks out of the exclusive country club. However, let us take an even closer look. Ephesians 2:1 states, "As for you, you were dead in your transgressions and sins." Romans 3:23 states, "All have sinned and come short of the glory of God." God is perfect. He has perfect justice. How can we, sinners living for our own desires, have a relationship with and live with God? Romans 8:34 says, "Who then is the one who condemns? No one." Whoa! No one? Jesus does not condemn us. He offers salvation as a gift. We choose to accept that gift or not. If we reject that gift, which we have the free will to do, then we condemn ourselves. We cannot blame anybody but ourselves. He will not force us to keep that gift. If you do not want it, that is your prerogative.

Imagine it is Christmas morning and, like a kid getting excited, we cannot wait to open our presents. We open one up and it is socks. We get disappointed and push it away. There are some people who would love to get socks. Socks may be the thing we need the most but we do not realize it. This is the way we treat a present from Jesus. Some love it. Some hate it. All need it. Without it, we condemn ourselves. We are keeping ourselves out of the country club.

We have to get rid of the sin if we hope to have that relationship with God. At first glance, it might look like we can do this through our good deeds. Maybe I can be good enough to get in. Unlike that earthly country club where we have to earn enough money, or be high enough on the social ladder, there is no way we can do enough good to get rid of our sin. If I commit murder, I cannot do good enough to erase that from my past. The cost of sin is too great, and we will never be able to afford it.

Others have told me life is not fair. Lynn Marie Sager, in *A River Worth Riding*, stated, "People are always complaining that life's not fair, but that simply isn't true. Life is extraordinarily fair. It's just not centered on you."[1] Truthfully, we should not want God to be fair. In fairness, we deserve death for our sins. In fairness, we deserve hell for our sins. Life may or may not be fair, but God is just. If a person breaks the law, and they receive no punishment, is that really justice? God's perfect justice cannot allow a sinful being a reward. It does not matter if you are a good person. It takes perfection, and no one is perfect. We all deserve punishment. It is not Jesus keeping us out. We are keeping ourselves out. So, is it possible to join this club?

We need a sacrifice. We need a person who has the capability to take that sin away. We need somebody who can pay the price of admittance. That price is the shed blood of the innocent. There is no other person on Earth that can take away our sins. There is nobody living that has not sinned and is innocent. The only person that could take our sins away is somebody who is not guilty of their own sins. We read in the Bible that Jesus was born of a virgin, led a sinless life, and died an innocent man. He is the only one who ever lived who was without sin.

The person would also have to do this freely. If they do not do this freely, then it is not a sacrifice. Jesus could have come down from the cross at any time. He chose to go to his death. He told his disciples he was going to his death. He knew it was going to happen and went toward it anyway. He did not run away. He chose to remain and die a miserable death so we

---

1. Sager, *River Worth Riding*, 17.

would have a chance to join the country club. John 3:17 states, "For God did not send his Son into the world to condemn the world, but to save the world through him." We were already condemned. We just needed a savior.

Jesus died on the cross to take away our sins. Only through him can we live in relationship with God. John 3:16 states, "For God so loved the world that he gave his one and only Son, that whoever believes in him shall not perish but have eternal life." When we put our trust in him, he puts a robe of righteousness on us. It covers our sins. All we have to do is believe in his life, death, and resurrection. We have to love Jesus and want to be in a relationship with him. We have to have enough faith in God to follow, and trust Jesus to take care of us. He will not force us. He loves us too much for that.

Christianity is different from other religions in the sense that we are saved not by the works we do but by the grace that he bestowed upon us. All that is asked of us is that we accept and love him. This is his desire from the very beginning. He does not want a slave. He wants a relationship.

This is so fantastic. It actually makes me happy knowing there is no work I can do to be saved. We do not have to shoot a good golf score and have a high social status to get in. We do not have to pay a bunch of money or be rich to remain.

Notice John 3:16 states *whoever*. In other words, anybody in the world can be included, if he or she wishes to be. It is not an exclusive country club but an inclusive country club.

The problem is that people keep pushing Jesus away. He is saying, "Just ask and I will give," but we keep saying no. We keep trying to earn our own way to heaven. If we do not want to live with him, we can choose otherwise. We are only keeping ourselves out. We do not have to do that. We keep performing works, thinking we will get on God's good side. It is as if we are thinking God is keeping score: if we do more good than bad, then we are in. We cannot do enough good. It takes perfection. We do not seem to realize we are already on God's good side. All we have to do is let him take care of us.

Do not misconstrue the message. I am not saying you have to ask Jesus to forgive you and then go on living your life as you wish. It is about a relationship. It is about falling in love. If we have that relationship, we will want to please him and put his wants before our wants. The relationship is about changing your heart. It is impossible to change our hearts ourselves. When we trust in Jesus, he transforms our heart, so that we are clean. It is about repentance, which means changing directions. You are no longer going your way, but Jesus' way. Do not ask me if I think you are going to heaven or not. I cannot judge that. Only Jesus knows because he is the only one who can see your heart and if you really care about him.

Do you love Jesus? Are you willing to just accept his free gift? If so, you too can join this country club. He is inviting all. He allows all who want.

CHAPTER 4

Chick-fil-A with Jesus

(Who Am I and Who Are You in This Relationship?)

BEV AND I WERE eating at Chick-fil-A one day. Right next to us was a young couple on their first date. I assumed they were on their first date. They were about high school age, dressed nice, and he was more nervous than a long-tailed cat in a room full of rocking chairs. We were also close enough to hear some of their conversation. I promise I was not stalking. They were asking typical questions to get to know each other, like "What type of music do you like?"

When you find somebody you want to date, it begins slowly. You might go out on a Friday or Saturday night, and it typically involves special events like going out to eat, seeing a movie, or going to a concert or museum. You find special things to do.

There are a couple of things you attempt to accomplish when you first start dating. First, you try to impress the other person. Typically, you want to come across as somebody interesting so your date will like you. You do not want to come across as a lazy bum with no ambitions and no future. In addition, you attempt to figure out if that person would be a good fit for you. You do this by asking questions to find out more about them. It is almost like a job interview. Today, you are applying to be my girlfriend. What do you have to offer?

The same thing happens when you start your relationship with Jesus. You might start out by going to church or going to special events like a concert. I call this the dating stage. In this stage, the relationship is selfish. We are attempting to see what we get from the other person that could make us happy. We ask questions about Jesus by praying and talking to mature Christians. We listen by reading his word and studying. What is Jesus like? Who is he? I started wondering what it would be like if we could sit across the table from Jesus, ask questions, and enjoy some Chick-fil-A.

Church: I like your outfit.

Jesus: Thank you, I have had these robes for a while but they are just so comfortable and they go great with the sandals.

Church: Do you like music?

Jesus: A person can wisely teach my message through psalms, hymns, and songs from the Spirit. Everyone should sing to God with gratitude in their hearts.[1] I have been known to sing a hymn before.[2]

Church: I know you are a great moral teacher; how do you feel about the state of society today?

Jesus: "What has been will be again, what has been done will be done again; there is nothing new under the sun."[3]

Church: I saw this church group protesting and saying God hates. I cannot believe they are Christians. I cannot believe God hates. It seems they are full of hate. I have been taught that God is love. Will you really take people like that to heaven?

Jesus: Sometimes people tend to look at others with righteous indignation. Whether you think they are doing right or wrong, "what is that to you? You must follow me."[4]

Church: We really try hard to make sure everybody knows we are accepting. It seems an attitude of not accepting is a problem in today's society.

Jesus: Acceptance at what level?

Church: Umm.

Jesus: Would you rather have love or acceptance?

Church: I would think if somebody loved me, he or she would accept me.

---

1. Col 3:16.
2. Mark 14:26.
3. Eccl 1:9.
4. John 21:22.

Jesus: If your three-year-old wants to play in the middle of the highway, do you let them?

Church: That would not seem very safe.

Jesus: What would you do?

Church: Probably force them to play somewhere else.

Jesus: Why?

Church: Because I care about them. I do not want them to get hurt.

Jesus: Would you say you love them?

Church: Yes, definitely.

Jesus: You love them, so you do not want to accept their behavior. Love and acceptance are not the same thing. Acceptance is great and desirable, but not at the expense of destruction.

Church: People seem so angry these days.

Jesus: Do you not get angry?

Church: Yes, but I am not perfect.

Jesus: We are not talking about hate. I do not want you to hate your neighbor. Having feelings of anger and jealousy is not bad in and of itself. I got angry with the sin of the moneychangers outside of the temple.[5] Did I do wrong? I have been known to get jealous because my people were cheating on me with idol worship.[6] Did I do wrong? Do you not understand that you have been created in the image of God?[7] You have been given those attributes to help you. When you see sin, it should make you angry. If your spouse cheats on you, you should feel jealousy. The problem is using those attributes to tear others down. I want you to use those attributes for good.

Church: Kids go up to Santa Claus and tell them how good they have been because they think Santa will give them a present. Some think of you that way. If they will be good, then you will give them what they want on Earth or take them to heaven someday. I just want it to go on record that I have been good for most of my life.

5. Matt 21:12.

6. Exod 34:14.

7. Gen 1:27.

Jesus: "No one is good-except God alone."[8] There is no one righteous, not even one.[9] Some people are always getting into trouble. "Blessed are the poor in Spirit, for theirs is the kingdom of heaven."[10]

Church: I am not sure I understand. Are you saying it is good if we do not have the Holy Spirit?

Jesus: The hardest to understand are the ones who do good works naturally. They look down on the troublemakers as if they were superior in some way. The poor in Spirit understand they need help. Therefore, they reach out, as they cannot do it on their own. Truth is, nobody can do it on their own. Understanding you are a sinner helps you understand your need for a Savior. They are blessed because they understand.

Church: My friend Cindy wanted me to have a relationship with you for a long time. She was a Christian. Honestly, for the longest time, I thought of you as a terrible person. Cindy died and we mourned hard. She was young, had three children, and had so much ambition for life. I tried to reach out to you and I asked you to save her, but she died.

Jesus: But I did save her.

Church: She died.

Jesus: I died on a cross to save her. I died on a cross to save you.

Church: No, I meant save her life so she could remain with us.

Jesus: So, you wanted me to save her twice.

Church: I could not understand how an all-powerful God could allow bad things to happen in this world.

Jesus: So if I would have healed her and let her live, you would have followed me and trusted in me?

Church: Yes!

Jesus: Is that true until the next bad thing happens? What happens when the next thing does not go your way?

Church: [pause]

8. Mark 10:18.

9. Rom 3:10.

10. Matt 5:3.

Jesus: Dying is just a part of living. There is so much more than living. "Blessed are those who mourn, for they will be comforted."[11]

Church: I am blessed if I am mourning? If I am mourning, I have lost, not gained.

Jesus: A person has to be allowed a free will, so evil will always exist. There is nothing wrong with mourning. Mourning just means you understand evil exists. Understanding evil exists makes one reach out and find what is important in life. People tend to turn to me when they have nowhere else to turn. No matter how bad the situation gets, I will always be there to comfort those who mourn.

Church: Well, you do like it when we work hard and do good, right?

Jesus: What I want is for everybody to "love the Lord your God with all your heart and will all your soul and with all your mind."[12] I would also like it if everybody would "love your neighbor as yourself."[13]

Church: You mean you do not care about how hard we work or the sacrifices we make?

Jesus: Surely, your work shows your love, but "obedience is greater than sacrifice."[14]

Church: I feel like my talents and intelligence would offer quite a bit to others.

Jesus: "Blessed are the meek, for they will inherit the Earth."[15]

Church: I am not sure I understand. On this Earth, the non-meek typically own everything. If you want something, you have to claw, fight, and backstab to get it. We could fight to make sure America has those morals you are wanting from us. If we do not fight, Christianity will lose. Are you saying we should not use our strengths?

---

11. Matt 5:4.
12. Matt 22:37.
13. Matt 22:39.
14. Jer 7:21–23.
15. Matt 5:5.

Jesus: "Blessed are those who hunger and thirst for righteousness."[16] You should want to be in right relationship with others and God. That certainly means helping others succeed. "Blessed are the merciful, for they will receive mercy."[17] Meek does not mean weak, tame, or deficient in courage. Each person has been given grace, so you should not think of yourself more highly than you ought to think.[18] Meek people are servants of God, willing to obey. It does not mean to deny your strengths but to use your strengths while understanding where you receive that strength. "You can do all things through me. It is I who gives you strength."[19] By the way, Christianity has already won, no matter what it looks like on Earth.

Church: I started asking people at work about you. I had people making fun of me. They think I am silly for even considering becoming a follower. I am afraid following you means giving up my dreams. It seems I either have to follow you and give up my dreams or follow my dreams and give you up. How can I have both?

Jesus: Why do you want both?

Church: I have worked hard to get where I am. I worked hard in school to get good grades. I went out of my way to accomplish certain goals. I cannot just give up all of that hard work.

Jesus: Working hard and learning is important but for what reason? Why should somebody want to be smart and work hard?

Church: I set goals to accomplish.

Jesus: Why do you think those goals are good?

Church: Society says I have to accomplish those goals to get what I want in life.

Jesus: What do you want in life?

Church: [Pause]

---

16. Matt 5:6.
17. Matt 5:7.
18. Rom 12:3.
19. Phil 4:13.

Jesus: What gives you satisfaction? Money? Prestige? Power? It is true those things can bring happiness, but it has been proven that happiness developed from those things will not last. "Happy are the people whose God is the Lord"![20] "He who heeds the word wisely will find good, and whoever trusts in the Lord, happy is he."[21] Therefore, "lay not up for yourselves treasures upon earth, where moth and rust doth corrupt, and where thieves break through and steal: but lay up for yourselves treasures in heaven, where neither moth nor rust doth corrupt, and where thieves do not break through nor steal: for where your treasure is, there will your heart be also."[22]

Church: I have seen what happened to the disciples. I know people around the world are tortured and even killed for believing in you.

Jesus: "Blessed are ye, when men shall revile you, and persecute you, and shall say all manner of evil against you falsely, for my sake. Rejoice, and be exceeding glad: for great is your reward in heaven: for so persecuted they the prophets which were before you."[23]

Church: I just do not know if I could go through something like that.

Jesus: "Blessed are those who are persecuted for righteousness' sake."[24]

Church: Are you really telling me I am blessed if I am persecuted? I cannot believe what I am hearing. I was always told a blessing is a good thing, but all I am hearing are bad things. I just do not understand.

Jesus: Why are all of these people blessed?

Church: [pause]

Jesus: How have they received a blessing?

Church: I am not sure.

Jesus: All of the people we have talked about are blessed because they are likely to find the relationship required for salvation. This life is short. "You are a mist that appears for a little while and then

---

20. Ps 144:15.
21. Prov 16:20.
22. Matt 6:19–21.
23. Matt 5:11–12.
24. Matt 5:10.

vanishes."[25] "Do not be afraid of those who kill the body but cannot kill the soul. Rather, be afraid of the One who can destroy both soul and body in hell."[26]

Church: [awkward pause]

Jesus: Tell me about you. Who are you?

Church: I consider myself to be strong, assertive, ready to fight, and a hard worker. It is starting to sound like that is not the type of person you are wanting. I am not sure a relationship would work between us.

Jesus: I think you would be perfect for this relationship.

Church: How?

Jesus: Who do you think you are to me?

Church: I am not sure.

Jesus: You are a friend.[27] You are loved.[28] You are blessed.[29] You are chosen.[30] You are forgiven.[31] You are a child of God.[32]

Church: Who are you?

Jesus: "Who do you say I am?"[33]

Church: I have heard you called a shepherd.

Jesus: I AM! "The good shepherd lays down his life for his sheep."[34]

Church: I have heard you called a prophet.

Jesus: I AM! A prophet is a messenger who is sent by and speaks for God.

Church: I have heard you called a priest.

---

25. Jas 4:14.
26. Matt 10:28.
27. John 15:15.
28. Rom 5:8.
29. Eph 1:3.
30. Eph 1:4.
31. 1 John 1:9.
32. Gal 3:26.
33. Matt 16:15.
34. John 10:11.

Jesus: I AM! A priest offers a sacrifice to atone for sins. "Without the shedding of blood there is no forgiveness of sins."[35] "I am the Great High Priest as I have offered the final, perfect sacrifice."[36]

Church: Some see you as a judge.

Jesus: I AM! I was appointed as judge of the living and the dead.[37]

Church: Some say you are a king.

Jesus: I AM! "I am the Lord of lords and King of kings. My kingdom is not of this world."[38]

Church: Who else are you?

Jesus: "I am the Alpha and Omega."[39] I am the head of the church.[40] I am the advocate.[41] I am the Messiah.[42] "I am the Lamb of God, who takes away the sin of the world."[43] I am Lord of all.[44] "I AM WHO I AM"![45]

Church: That was a good meal. Do you want to get out of here?

Jesus: Sure.

Church: The garden down the road has a nice winding walking path. Would you want to go for a walk?

Jesus: No, I have not had good experiences in gardens[46] or on winding, predefined paths. I prefer straight and narrow ways.[47] I am going

---

35. Heb 9:22.
36. Heb 10:14.
37. Acts 10:42.
38. John 18:36.
39. Rev 22:13.
40. Eph 1:22.
41. 1 John 2:1.
42. John 1:41.
43. John 1:29.
44. Phil 2:9–11.
45. Exod 3:14.
46. John 18:1–12.
47. Matt 7:13–14.

to go for now. I have to go see my Father.[48] Do not fear, I will be back, and we can be together.[49]

Church: Thank you for taking time to talk with me.

Jesus: It was my pleasure.

48. John 14:2.
49. John 14:3.

CHAPTER 5

Falling in Love

(It Is Not a Chore)

AFTER YOU HAVE BEEN dating for a little while, you begin to learn whether this is a person you want to trust. You learn if you want to be around this person more frequently. If so, you might start finding extra time to see them. The relationship goes beyond a formal, occasional dating, to a more frequent, casual interaction.

The more we dated, the more I found I wanted to be around Bev, my future wife. I used to work until about six in the evening, so by the time I got off it was too late to do something big. It gets too expensive to do special events all of the time, but I still wanted to be around Bev. Couples might end up just hanging out and talking or watching a television show or movie from home. It is typically a more relaxed atmosphere, but you also spend much more time with the other person. Bev and I used to take walks, ending up at the convenience store, getting a drink, maybe a candy treat, and walking back home.

I call this stage in the relationship process enlightenment. At this stage of the relationship, the attitudes are changing. You start telling each other secrets that you do not tell others. Plans are created. Vulnerability ensues. You get to know one another very well. It is here that you become a stable couple. It is here that you develop that committed relationship. It is here that you fall in love.

I see the same thing happening with our relationship with Jesus. We wish to learn more about him so we start reading more, both the Bible and Christian books, and watching YouTube videos and other material. We get together with other Christians more frequently to help us build our faith. We pray more, talking to Jesus. We are no longer in a relationship that is formal and occasional. I remember some Christians I looked up to as a kid and they would talk to Jesus as if he was their best friend. At this point, we have moved on to a more frequent, casual interaction. A long time ago, they would call this "going steady," or dating exclusively. It is here we get to know Jesus very well. Our attitudes are changing. The process is progressing. We are growing closer. We are becoming enlightened. We are falling in love.

As the love grows, you start to do special things for the other person again, but in a different way. You might look for opportunities to be romantic or find a way to show that other person you love them. Maybe you buy them flowers. Maybe you go out of your way to show them how much you love them. There was this time I gave Bev a clue and sent her on a scavenger hunt. She solved many clues and at the end found a special present.

The reason you do this is your love for them, and not because it is a requirement to stay in the relationship. Did you catch that? At first, we do things in the relationship because we are selfish and want to impress the other person. We are hoping to get love. As we fall in love, we do things in the relationship because we care about the other person more than we do ourselves. We are hoping to give love. In the process, giving means getting because it makes us happy.

I will never forget the first time Bev cooked me dinner. She fixed roast, potatoes, and carrots in the crockpot. I do not know why she cooked me dinner. Maybe our relationship had reached a new stage. Maybe she thought our relationship was in a position where we started to view each other with the eye of living together for the rest of our lives. Maybe she wanted me to see her as a person who can take care of my needs through food. I do like food.

The reason I will never forget the first time she cooked for me was because of the joke that would soon follow. Shortly after, I had to go to the doctor over a pain in the center of my abdomen. Turns out, I had gallstones, requiring surgery to remove the gallbladder. Her cooking a meal for me would not have caused this to happen but that did not mean I was not going to blame her. By this time, we had grown close enough for me to joke about my medical problems being her fault. Even today, I tell people how her first time cooking for me sent me to the hospital.

Although she was already telling me she loved me at this time, you still wonder what that means. Is she using the word "love" because it is the socially correct thing to do? Is she saying she loves me because I have told her I love her? There is nothing that lets a person know how much another loves them until they see it in action.

The day of surgery came and the operation went smoothly. I was in some pain and was required to stay in the hospital overnight. My family was there and so was Bev. After some time, lying in the bed, I developed a small problem. It really was not a big deal but, as a typical man, I am a big baby and I turned it into something bigger. My family left. The nurses decided to take action against my small problem. I was in pain and I felt alone. Then I realized that Bev was still there. She was the only one still there. She held me. She encouraged me. She sat by my bedside until I felt good again. She was there for hours into the night.

Those are the times you understand how much they really love you. Our relationship had reached a new stage. It was about caring for the other person more than ourselves. I call this stage commitment, and I view true love as the time when you desire the wants and needs of others before your own. I grew to understand this even more as our daughter came into our lives. I have gone through extraordinary situations because of that love— situations I never would have considered in my youth. Love is more than a feeling that comes over you at a given time. Love is a choice we make to care for others in the way we want them to care for us.

Sitting in that hospital is not something fun. It is not something she wanted to do. She did not sit there because it was a task that was expected of her. She did not feel obligated as if it was some required chore. She did it because she cared about me. She loved me enough to want to make sure I was going to be okay. It was not about her. It was about me.

There are different ways to show another person you love him or her. You might share intimate feelings or thoughts with them only. A person can show they love another by just being honest. You can show romantic gestures like buying flowers or creating a special event. All of that is great, but nothing shows love like standing by your partner in bad times. Standing by them in good times is easy. Standing by them in bad times is one hundred times greater. Showing your love is about caring enough to please their desires.

The same thing happens as we fall in love with Jesus. John 14:15 states, "If you love me, keep my commands." It is so easy for an outsider to read that and say that Christianity is about following a bunch of commands. They might see God as a dictator saying, "Keep my commands, or else bad things will come upon you." This is not what Christianity is. They are forgetting to see the first part of that verse. What they do not see is that we have fallen in love. I did not command Bev to stay with me in the hospital, but she knew I wanted it. Bev stood by me because she knew it would help me, and she loved me enough to be unselfish and actually help.

As we view the commands of God, what are we really looking at? We should see those commands as something we desire. Not because God orders us to, but because our hearts want to please him. Our love flows harder than the work.

Do you think living a Christian life is hard? It can be! Some think chasing God is hard because of what they will lose. They might have to leave their so-called good friends. They might have to change from their so-called good job. They might not want to give up the so-called nice things they enjoy. What they are not seeing is what they will gain. The key is finding our love for Jesus. When we are immature, we might be able to see the love Jesus has for us, but when we find our love for Jesus, the relationship becomes perfect. We cannot expect a love relationship to go just one way. To work, it has to be mutual. Being in a relationship with God will not only affect your eternity, but it will make your earthly life greater as well. The more you get to know God, the more like Christ you become, and your life becomes fulfilling.

The Bible is a special revelation given to us to show us who God is. It is the story of Jesus. Through it, as well as through general revelation, we learn what Jesus likes and dislikes. We do not do the things he likes because it is fun. We do not stay away from his dislikes because it is a required chore. We behave this way because we desire to please him more than please ourselves. We have fallen in love. Without that love, it would be an excruciating relationship. Once you find that love, Christianity is no longer difficult.

James 2:17 states, "Faith by itself, if it does not have works, is dead." This confuses many people because works do not save us. James was telling us that if we love Jesus, we want to do things for him. Not because of some requirement, or because working for him will get us into heaven, or anything else that is selfish, but because we care about him. Working for him is just a by-product of our love for him.

Christianity is not about following a bunch of rules. Other religions are about following rules. I have literally heard people of other faiths state that their religion is about doing more good than bad. Christianity is about a relationship with a person. A real person who roamed the Earth two thousand years ago. As the relationship grows, we want to do more and more for that other person. Soon we are doing things for them, not because we are expected to perform an unpleasant chore, or that we may receive some reward for our effort, but because it pleases us to make them happy. As we look at the commands of God, we see there are only two things he wants. He wants us to put him first, giving him our hearts, and then love other people.

Jesus took our sins with him when he went to the cross. We look at the cross and think of how terrible it must have been, and I am sure it was. However, the writer of Hebrews shows us a different view. Hebrews 12:2 states, "Look to Jesus, the founder and perfecter of our faith, who for the joy that was set before him endured the cross, despising the shame, and is seated at the right hand of the throne of God."

Did I read that right? Did Jesus have joy going to the cross? Not exactly. He knew, to get what he desired, he had to endure the pain of the cross. There was no other way to accomplish his goals. He desires to have a close relationship with us. He desires us in paradise. It is the very reason for creating us. The only way to have this relationship was to take our sins away. The only way to do this was to have a sinless sacrifice take our place. He was the only one who could do it. He loved us so much, he would go through that great unpleasantness to reach that goal. Could you just imagine? What if the only way to be with your spouse was to take on some incredible punishment? Do you love them that much? That is how much Jesus loved us. He wanted to be in a relationship with us so much that he literally took the punishment.

To a lesser degree, it is similar to Bev sitting in that hospital room against her own comfort. Eventually an event is going to pop up that is going to test the amount of love you have for Jesus. John 16:33 states, "I have told you these things, so that in me you may have peace. In this world you will have trouble. But take heart! I have overcome the world." This trouble will come in various forms and degrees. Some may experience a few very small problems, while others may experience many huge problems, but make no mistake about it, problems are going to come. When it does, where will you be? Will you be there to support the relationship? Will you be gone because you care more about your wants than the wants of Jesus?

When you have been married for as long as Bev and I have, you get to know each other. Bev knows me very well. She even knows some things about me I wish she did not. There is good, there is bad, and there is ugly. I love her to see the good. I wish that is all she saw from me. She knows the bad. She has seen the ugly. She continues to love me through it all.

Jesus knows 100 percent of us. We would love it if he only saw our good but he sees it all. He has seen the bad. He understands the ugly, yet he still loves us. As that ugly sin keeps me in my metaphoric hospital bed, he loves me so much he stays with me. He never leaves me. He holds me. He comforts me. He died to take away the ugly. What am I willing to do for him? What are you willing to do for him?

By the way, Bev is a great cook. Roast, potatoes, and carrots in the crockpot is one of my favorite dishes. She knows I love her.

CHAPTER 6

The Spaghetti Offense
(Learning to Judge Correctly)

I AM A TERRIBLE cook. If I have to cook, I usually look in the freezer and see what I can microwave. Even then, you probably would not want to eat it.

Growing up, my mother had her usual dishes. We would typically see the same meals every week. They just became staples. I think that is typical in most households. One of those meals was spaghetti.

When you are young, spaghetti just does not make sense. First, the child cannot pronounce the word, calling it "pasghetti." Then, they cannot eat it without getting messy. Long noodles hang out of their mouth. Slurping takes place. It is not for those times when you have company over. Why do we continue to fix this sloppy food? Well, it tastes good, it is easy to fix, most people like it, and it is cheap. Therefore, I do not see spaghetti dinners disappearing anytime soon.

Since spaghetti was going to be cooked, my parents taught me how to eat it and not make a mess. They decided to show me how to cut it up into smaller bites. Cutting spaghetti is not like cutting a piece of meat. If you do not trap the spaghetti, the noodles just slide back and forth on the plate. Therefore, when I would cut it, I would trap the noodles between the fork and knife and slice. The slicing would make a scraping noise as the knife ran along the side of the fork and plate. I would do this to the entire plate, and in a matter of seconds, the pieces would be so small, they would be bite-sized instead of long noodles. Yay! No more mess.

When I married Bev, she did not want my patented microwaved frozen food. She decided to do the cooking. Bev is a great cook. She also liked to fix spaghetti. Since I grew up cutting my spaghetti, and had done so for the last twenty years, I did not think much about it as an adult. Maybe I should have. I continued this slicing technique. After a few times of eating spaghetti, my wife changed it up. She no longer served me the long noodles. She would use the same sauce but use short pasta like bowtie, elbow, rotini, penne, etc. This went on for a long time. I never gave it a second thought.

One day we were going to have spaghetti. Bev cooked the meal, we sat down to eat, and I noticed we were not eating the same thing. I had short pasta noodles and she had long spaghetti noodles. My curiosity got the best of me. Why would she fix two different kinds of pasta noodles? Does that not take an easy-to-fix meal and make it harder? Turns out, she wanted long spaghetti noodles. Wait. What? Why did she not just fix the one kind then? Turns out, she did not want me eating long noodles. Okay, what is up? She told me the scraping of the fork and knife together, when I cut my spaghetti, drove her crazy. I never knew that. She said it was like fingernails on a chalkboard. For the longest time afterwards, she would fix two different pastas on spaghetti night.

This brings up many difficult questions. Did I create an offense to my wife? Merriam-Webster defines offense as "something that outrages the moral or physical senses"; "the act of displeasing"; or "an infraction of law."[1] I tried to make the defense that I did not know I was offending her. That really did not matter. Although I did not know I was offending, it was still offensive.

Have you ever heard the legal system say ignorance of the law is no excuse? Once we were driving in Indiana, when a police officer pulled me over for speeding. We had a chat and I ended up receiving a ticket. I am one who tries to follow the law, even if I think the authorities are not watching. What made me mad was that I did not know what the speed limit was. We were in a different state, and I had not seen a speed limit sign. Maybe I missed it somewhere. I was still guilty of speeding. I still broke the law or created an offense.

Merriam-Webster defines sin as "an offense against religious or moral law," or "transgression of the law of God."[2] Can somebody commit a sin and not understand they are sinning? Parts of the Bible seem to indicate you can. King David said in Psalm 19:12, "Forgive my hidden faults." In this passage, David is asking God for forgiveness, and he understands he may

1. Merriam-Webster, "Offense."
2. Merriam-Webster, "Sin."

have sinned unknowingly. It would seem logical that we would not know everything, especially when we are young and immature.

Does this mean we are guilty of the sin? YES! There is no way to be perfect. Just living life means you are going to mess up. Leviticus 5:17 states, "If anyone sins and does what is forbidden in any of the Lord's commands, even though they do not know it, they are guilty and will be held responsible." Whoa! Wait! What? It tells us we are guilty and responsible even if we do not understand our offense. Just like me having to pay that speeding ticket, we have to pay for our sins. Should we be held accountable for sins of which we are not aware? That cannot be fair, can it?

Before we answer that question, let us step back for a moment and remind ourselves of what saves us. There is no amount of work we can accomplish to attain salvation. There is no amount of money because the cost is too great. We needed a perfect sacrifice, and that came through the atoning blood of Jesus Christ. He lived a perfect life, died on the cross an innocent man, and arose three days later, conquering death. Salvation became an act of grace on the part of Jesus, and is attained through faith on our part.

Back to the topic. Romans 2:12 states, "All who have sinned without the law will also perish without the law, and all who have sinned under the law will be judged by the law." In other words, yes, you are held accountable. You will perish even if you have never heard of the law.

Before you say that is not fair, I want you to keep the whole thing in perspective. If we are saved by grace through faith in Jesus Christ, then keeping the law is not what saves us. So, why did God give us the law in the first place? Romans 3:19–20 states, "Now we know that whatever the law says it speaks to those who are under the law, so that every mouth may be stopped, and the whole world may be held accountable to God. For by works of the law no human being will be justified in his sight, since through the law comes knowledge of sin." There it is. We are already sinners. The law is given to *show us* we are sinners. That is *all* it does. Without perfection, we cannot have a relationship with God. When we realize we are not perfect, we can understand our need for a savior. Realizing our need offers us the opportunity to ask for help or choose to reject, as desired.

At this point, you might be saying that this still does not answer the question of never hearing the law. Maybe a person grew up in an isolated tribe in the Amazon. Correct, but Paul did not leave anybody out. Romans 1:19–20 states, "Since what may be known about God is plain to them, because God has made it plain to them. For since the creation of the world God's invisible qualities—his eternal power and divine nature—have been clearly seen, being understood from what has been made, so that people are without excuse." Romans 2:15 states, "The requirements of the law are written on their hearts, their consciences also bearing witness, and their thoughts sometimes accusing them and at other times even defending them." Paul is speaking about the gentiles who do not have the law. God and his laws are made known to us without the Bible.

This does not mean we understand all of the many laws on the Jewish books. We do not have to know all of those laws. Jesus said the greatest law was to love God and the second was to love your neighbor. All laws fall into those two categories. Our conscience tells us how to love God and love others.

As we grow, we naturally learn moral and ethical principles. At some point, of which I do not know, the Holy Spirit convicts us. Conviction is the understanding that we are guilty and God is calling us to him. Since following the law does not save you, knowing you have done wrong leads you to God. James 2:10 states, "For whoever keeps the whole law and yet stumbles at just one point is guilty of breaking all of it." It does not matter how many laws we know. Just one thing wrong should lead you on a hunt for God, and we have all done at least one thing wrong. Romans 3:23 states, "All have sinned and fall short of the glory of God."

Now, it would seem, since we have the Bible, sin would be black and white. There are sins that seem obvious offenses to God. However, some sin can have the appearance of being subjective. In the Gospel of Matthew, chapter 19, a man comes to Jesus and tells him how he has followed the law all of his life and wants to know what else he has to do to be saved. Nowhere in the Bible does God say you have to be poor to have salvation. Jesus does say it is hard for a rich man to enter heaven, but he never says it's impossible.[3] The terms "rich" and "poor" are subjective anyway. Here, Jesus tells him to go and sell all of his possessions and the man goes away sad. Why? He did not want a changed heart. It was easy for him to keep the written law. He kept all of the law and still could not attain salvation. Why? Salvation comes through faith, not works. Jesus found that one thing in this man's life that kept his heart from transforming.

What is faith? Hebrews 11 tells us that "faith is confidence in what we hope for and assurance about what we do not see." Faith is about believing

---

3. Matt 19:24.

in God's ability to save us, knowing he will keep his promises, and as a result, being willing to follow him, wherever he leads, because we trust him.

Hebrews 11 lists Old Testament saints and tells us they were saved by faith. The ancients believed God would provide. Even Adam and Eve were given a promise of a future savior. In Genesis 3:15, right after they mess up, God tells them a future savior is coming to correct the sin problem. They had no idea of who Jesus was. They had faith that God would accomplish what he told them, so their faith led them to follow him, wherever that meant. They made their mistakes, but they had enough faith to follow. The Old Testament saints, like Abraham, Moses, Noah, etc., made their mistakes, but they had enough faith to follow. In the New Testament, we see the disciples making mistakes, but they still had enough faith to follow. That is what he is asking from us. He is calling out to us and he is telling us to follow. We are going to make mistakes, and he understands this, but we need to have faith in the atoning work of Christ. We need to have faith that he will follow through with his promises, and in faith, we will follow him wherever he leads.

Is this not what happens in any relationship? When I got married, I did not think I would never mess up in my marriage. I have messed up many times. I did not tell Bev to go one way and I would go another. We are in a covenant relationship, so we work as a team. I will always go anywhere with my wife and do anything to make our marriage good.

When you ask Jesus to be a part of your life, and you enter into a sacred covenant with him, he will transform your heart. We have to have the faith it takes to follow. Romans 14:23 states, "Whatever does not proceed from faith is sin."

Therefore, this is where I am going to argue slightly with Merriam-Webster. I think they left something out of their definition of sin. Sin can be *anything* that draws us away from making God first in our lives. It is an inward heart issue. The thing that we personally struggle with, and that keeps us from making him number one in our lives, is what becomes sin for us. For some it may mean murder—or hate in your heart. For some it may be adultery—or lust in your heart. Maybe it is gossip—or mean-spiritedness in your heart. You can name your sin here.

Since sin is a heart issue, we cannot judge another person's relationship with God. We can discern right and wrong and help our fellow Christians understand God better, but we cannot see what is going on in their brain. We may look good on the outside but be a disappointment to God.

The Pharisees followed the law and Jesus told the people they had to be more righteous than the Pharisees. We may also look bad on the outside, according to others, and be pleasing to God. We cannot be perfect and follow the law perfectly, but we can have a relationship with Christ and be made perfect by him.

This brings up another question. If sin can be subjective, can an act be a sin for one and not another? Do you remember the person in the book of Matthew who would not give up his money? It was a sin for *him* to have money but not for others. In 1 Corinthians, Paul is asked about eating meat that has been offered to idols. Paul shows them we have freedom in Christ to do what we want, and since there really are no other gods, we are free to eat that meat.

However, since sin is a heart issue, if you believe eating the meat is sinful, then eating the meat for you is sin. We have similar struggles. I am free to drink alcohol, but if you believe drinking alcohol is sin, then for you it is a sin. You cannot just do what you want. We have to honestly search God's desires and let that guide us. In doing this, we show God we love him.

There is also something more important than a person's freedoms and rights. In whatever we do, we need to show love. Do you remember the other commandment to love your neighbor? You have freedom to eat the meat, but if eating the meat might cause somebody to stumble in their faith, then do not eat the meat. I am free to drink alcohol, but if drinking alcohol causes another to stumble in their faith, then I do not drink alcohol. We worry so much about our constitutional rights that we lose sight of the bigger picture. It is not about me having free speech. It is about treating my neighbor respectfully. It is not about the freedom of press. It is about lifting others to Jesus.

Last question. Why did Bev not divorce me, since I created an offense against her? Wait, Rick. That is only an offense with spaghetti. That is not doing something bad like cheating on her. So what! The greatness of the sin is only a human concept. How about humankind destroyed because Adam and Eve could not resist a piece of fruit? Is eating fruit a sin? Not for most people, but it is if God tells you to not eat a piece of fruit.

I am going to make an argument. You may think differently about this. It depends on how you define sin. I think sin existed before Adam and Eve ate the fruit. The sin was in their heart. The real sin of Adam and Eve was not an outward act of eating but an inward heart issue of greed. We do not have a timeline but I am guessing they stared at the tree for a long time before they went for it. Even if it was a short time, they coveted, which breaks one of the Ten Commandments. They wanted more than God had given them. They wanted to be equal in knowledge with God. Sin existed before they ate the fruit. They just did not understand their sin. God gave them a law of not eating the fruit to help them understand their hearts as flawed, or sinful. Once they ate, they could finally understand their sin.

Bev did not divorce me because our marriage is not based on our works. Our marriage is based on our love for one another. Our covenant with Jesus is not based on works either. It is based on grace, faith, and love. Now, as a by-product, my love for my wife causes me to serve her, but our marriage is not based on it, and she is not going to just throw me out because I mess up. Neither will God.

This is tricky theology because they go hand in hand. This does not mean I can keep offending. One day, after at least twenty-four years of marriage (not exaggerating), Bev fixed long spaghetti noodles for both of us. I was speechless. Knowing the cutting offended her, I took my fork, grabbed a little spaghetti, moved it to the side of the plate, and rolled it on my fork. After I understood the offense, my love for her made me change my ways. To not change shows a lack of love. It shows a lack of caring. My love for her makes me want to please her. Once I understand the offense, I need to change my ways.

In the same way, our love for God should make us want to follow his desires. In Romans chapter 6, Paul explains that we cannot go on sinning. Accepting him means dying to our sin. Hebrews 10:26 states, "If we deliberately keep on sinning after we have received the knowledge of the truth, no sacrifice for sins is left." In other words, you are damaging the relationship. We cannot suppress the truth in order to keep sinning as we wish. If we love Jesus, we will do what he wants us to do, no matter where that leads.

CHAPTER 7

Seeing Is Not Believing

(The Subtle Deceptions of Satan)

THROUGHOUT MY LIFE, I have had to deal with several instances of ethical and moral decisions. I was taught it was not right to lie and cheat. After all, was that not the idea behind our parents telling us the story of the boy who cried wolf?

I am always telling myself to not be afraid of the truth. The reason I do this is that I am afraid my bias will influence me to follow something false, because I want it to be that way. Therefore, I try to follow a path of logic.

When I was a young man, I found a job unloading the fifty-three-foot semi-trailer for a large department store. We would take the boxes off the trailer, unpack the inventory, and put it on the shopping floor or stack it in the stockroom. I remember this one time we were going through an audit. An independent auditor would observe the operation and count the materials coming into the store. My boss pulled me aside and told me to sneak boxes past the auditor if they were not looking. By doing this, that particular store in the chain would look better than it really was.

I wish people could just be honest. It is not hard to follow the rules. My experience has been that it takes more work to cheat, steal, and lie. You also feel guilty and depressed. When situations like this arise, decisions have to be made. Do I act unethically and lie, following the orders of my boss, or do I stand firm on the moral high ground, telling the truth, and hope I do not get fired? Moments such as these make a person's life more stressful than it needs to be. It was not fair for my boss to put me in that situation. It is not fair for any boss to put their employee in those situations. I did not want to lose my job. My family was counting on me to take care of them. As stressful as that can be, I have never had to deal with something like having to lie to decide between life and death. Therefore, I attempt to keep my thoughts in context and consider my life issues to be a bit simplistic.

There are places around the world where being a Christian means danger. It could mean prison, being beaten, and even death. These people have serious, stressful decisions to make. Do they stand up for the truth and continue to follow and teach Jesus, or do they lie and hide the truth in an effort to stay safe?

Early Christians had some tough decisions to make as well. They wanted to tell people the good news, but the leaders of that time wanted it stopped. The Christians understood the risks involved as they had already seen people killed in the name of Jesus. The Bible records these martyrs. They included Stephen and John the Baptist. Do they stop spreading the news because the leadership is forcing them? Do they lie to save their own lives, or risk death?

The leaders of the early church recorded what happened to all of the disciples and apostles. We have information from Papias, Clement of Rome, Polycarp, Iranaeus, Clement of Alexandria, Hippolytus, Tertullian, Origen, Eusebius, Jerome, and others. When we read this history, we find out that all of the disciples and apostles were either tortured or killed for their belief in Jesus. They were beheaded, crucified, beaten to death, hanged, stabbed, and stoned. The only one to survive to live a long life, although still persecuted, was John. John was boiled in a huge basin of oil. He survived. Then he was exiled to the island of Patmos. By the way, John did some great work for Jesus after being exiled.

These people were not doing bad things. They did not gain power or money because they converted from Judaism to Christianity. Just the opposite happened. They died just because of their belief in Jesus. They did not have an earthly motive to follow Jesus but had earthly motives to deny Jesus. Some of these, like Paul and Jesus' brother James, already had high positions in society. They gave those up to follow Jesus.

Why would somebody die when they could change their story and save their own life? Changing their story is exactly what the disciples did prior to the resurrection of Jesus. The disciples did not fully understand yet and were afraid. Matthew 26:35 states, "But Peter declared, 'Even if I have to die with you, I will never disown you.' And all the other disciples said the same." Peter said he would die for Jesus, but just a short time after he made this statement, he denied being a follower three separate times. He was confronted by the people and was afraid for his life. Matthew says all of the disciples said they would die for Jesus, yet they all scattered. This was actually prophecy being fulfilled from Zech 13:7–9. The disciples forsook Jesus and scattered.

Why did the disciples deny and scatter? They were scared they would lose their lives. With their leader dead, they now doubted what they understood to be truth. They told Jesus they would stand for him when they thought Jesus could do anything. Peter was even ready to fight with his sword before they arrested Jesus. As they watched Jesus die, their attitudes changed. They were no longer willing to die because they doubted and probably thought it was false all along.

After the resurrection, we see a different story. Peter is now willing to die and never again deny the name of Jesus. Paul changed from Christian persecutor to complete follower willing to die for his belief. James, the brother of Jesus, changed his belief and he ended up dying for it. All of the disciples did a 180-degree turn and suffered in the name of Jesus. Something big had to happen to make this change in them.

For the longest time I thought that it was their belief that gave them the courage to die for their cause. The followers went from skeptical to full belief. Notice how much the word "belief" is coming up. This fundamental change in their lives was evidence for me and gave me encouragement that Christianity was true. They were only willing to die because they truly believed. Their faith gave them the courage it took to face death.

Then one day I was talking with a friend. We were talking about this idea of them facing death. I said it shows evidence that Christianity is true. Then he brought to my attention that people all over the world die for things they believe. They are not all Christians. We, in America, saw this on September 11, 2001, when terrorists killed thousands of people in New York and Washington, DC. People all over the world are willing to die for their beliefs. They might be from other religions or political backgrounds. Just because a person is willing to die for their belief does not mean their religion is true.

This bugged me for quite some time because the disciples and apostles dying for their belief seemed like such strong evidence to show others the truth, but seeing all of the Muslims dying for their belief had me taking a closer look. Was I thinking illogically? Was I using this thought as evidence when I should not have been? I had to face the truth. It is logical, and I want to follow logic. I had to face the facts. Martyrdom is not a confirmation of truth, but rather a confirmation of what an individual believes to be true.

Then, one day, I was reading a book by Lee Strobel entitled *The Case for Christ*.[1] He had an interview that covered this exact topic. He showed how it was not necessarily their belief that allowed them to become martyrs but that they saw and touched Jesus, which made their faith tangible. Did you notice the subtle difference? As I was reading, suddenly it felt like a ton of bricks had fallen on me. I felt so stupid that I had let my friend use logical-sounding words to lead me away from the truth, and I was grateful to Strobel for pointing me back in the right direction.

There is a well-known phrase that says, "Seeing is believing." It suggests skepticism. It implies that we cannot know the truth unless we see it. The problem is that it does not take faith or belief if we see it. John 20:29 states, "Then Jesus told him, 'Because you have seen me, you have believed; blessed are those who have not seen and yet have believed.'" Jesus was telling them that it does not take faith for them to believe in the resurrection because they saw him. It takes faith in the resurrection if you have not seen him.

Seeing is not believing. It takes belief if we do not see it. I, personally, have to either believe or not believe in the resurrection of Jesus because I did not see it with my own eyes. If I saw it, I would know it to be true.

If the disciples never saw Jesus resurrected, they would not have believed it to be true. More than likely, they would have thought the Romans took his body somewhere else. We have proof of this. Thomas, after being told he had risen, could not believe it. He was not going to believe unless he saw Jesus alive.

Going back, we saw the disciples scatter because they were afraid for their lives. They stopped believing in Jesus when they saw him crucified. Yet, the church records the lives and deaths of the apostles, and they were persecuted for preaching, teaching, and leading others to Jesus. Thomas preached Jesus to the people, until his death by spear.

Here is the kicker. The argument is that people will die for what they believe in, but they are not willing to die for a stance they think is false. The resurrection witnesses did not have to believe like you and I do. Logic would say they died horrible deaths because they knew it to be true. Seeing is not believing. Seeing is knowing, and the apostles died because they witnessed it and it changed them completely. They saw him alive!

---

1. Strobel, *Case for Christ*, 247.

That is one evidence that helps me understand Christianity as truth. Without the resurrection, I would not believe in Jesus Christ as the savior of the world. If nobody ever saw him alive, why would I ever believe he rose from the dead? Seeing and touching him gave them the courage to handle the persecution. First Corinthians 15:6 states, "After that, he appeared to more than five hundred of the brothers and sisters at the same time, most of whom are still living, though some have fallen asleep." Christianity is based on the salvation work of Jesus, but history tells us the story, and the future owes these saints a tremendous thank you. I can believe because they knew the truth.

It is so important that we have the truth grounded in us so that we mature in Christ and do not allow people to lead us astray. Without understanding, we are risking our relationship with God. We risk allowing those logical-sounding arguments to consume us and pull us away from the truth.

I am not attempting to create an apologetic argument for the resurrection of Jesus. I am trying to show the way Satan works. It is important to understand. He uses words that sound so logical and desirable that they draw us away before we even know what has happened to us. Think about Adam and Eve. Surely, you will not die just for eating a piece of fruit.[2] Sounds logical. Adam and Eve had a close relationship with God, yet they were tempted to stray. How? Through logical-sounding, flesh-desiring, lack-of-understanding deceitfulness. Satan's words sounded logical, yet humanity suffered for the act of Adam.

Do not get me wrong, I am a fan of logic. What I am not a fan of is subtle, false statements that sound logical but are actually misleading. Timothy states, "There will be terrible times in the last days. People will be lovers of themselves, lovers of money, boastful, proud, abusive, disobedient to their parents, ungrateful, unholy, without love, unforgiving, slanderous, without self-control, brutal, not lovers of the good, treacherous, rash, conceited, lovers of pleasure rather than lovers of God—having a form of godliness but denying its power."[3] Did he leave anybody out? Do you think these people just wake up one day and say they have decided to be treacherous and rash? No way! It took subtle lies over a long period. To get from point A to point B may take hundreds of years and several small deceptions. I

2. Gen 3:3–5.

3. 2 Tim 3:1–5.

think many people will be destroyed believing they are doing what they think is right.

There are tons of examples of this in our world today. There are those who say there is no absolute truth. There are those that say love should conquer all and that means accepting their behavior. There are those that paint God as a tyrant because of what they have read in the Old Testament. There are those who point out that Jesus said he was coming back soon, and it is false since it is two thousand years later and it still has not happened. There are many subtle lies. All of these logical-sounding errors draw us away from the truth. All of them pull us away from what is important. There is nobody better at this deception than Satan. Isaiah states, "Woe unto them that call evil good, and good evil; that put darkness for light, and light for darkness; that put bitter for sweet, and sweet for bitter! Woe unto them that are wise in their own eyes, and prudent in their own sight!"[4] Satan has a way of fooling us. It is not because we want to be bad, but because we think we are pursuing good and quit following the standard God has set.

The way Satan works reminds me of an old *Saturday Night Live* (*SNL*) skit I called Land Shark. It is about a shark who has the capability of walking on land, looking for food. The Land Shark knocks on a person's door. The resident asks who is there, and he says, "Land Shark." Sometimes the resident opens their door thinking it must be some sort of a joke. When they open their door, the Land Shark eats them. When somebody says they are not going to open the door to a Land Shark, he changes it to something else more desirable, like "pizza delivery." Then he still eats them when they open their door. The ridiculousness of the skit makes it funny, but there is nothing funny about Satan's subtle deceptions. Satan does not ring our doorbell and say, "It is Satan. I am here to take you to hell." Who would open the door if they heard that? He subtly changes the truth to sound appealing. Ding-dong, "Basket of puppies!" Then once you open the door, there is a basket of puppies, but they turn out to be vicious, ravenous creatures, ready to eat your face.

The subtle lies that spread are the work of Satan. It is these subtle, logical-sounding lies that prevent people from having a relationship with Jesus Christ. It is these subtle, logical-sounding lies that pull people out of the church. Be careful when you talk to others. Do not let them convince you into thinking differently about the truth. Do not let Satan deceive you with his subtleties. Study God's word and place it in your heart. Deuteronomy

4. Isa 5:20–21.

11:18 states, "You shall therefore lay up these words of mine in your heart and in your soul." Trust in God, knowing his ways are true, and follow Christ wholeheartedly.

SECTION 2

The Engaged Life

CHAPTER 8

The Sacrifice

(Surrendering Your Life for the Cause of Christ)

BEV AND I DID not date for a long time before we decided to get married. The purpose of the dating process is to find somebody with whom you would like to spend the rest of your life. Once you have dated for a sufficient amount of time, you should be able to make this determination. We ask the other person to become a part of our lives.

The same thing happens with God. After we have fallen in love with Jesus, we make a determination as to whether we want to be in a committed relationship with him. Making this commitment is like engagement. What does it mean to commit your lives to each other? What does that look like?

When I was younger, I played tennis almost every day. I loved it. I watched the sport on television and attended a couple of professional tournaments. I can even remember cleaning snow off the court to play. As I have aged, I must have gotten lazy. I never make it out to the courts anymore. Instead, I prefer less active games, such as chess. I am not sure you can find a game or sport with as little activity involved. You literally sit in one place and just think.

I love the game of chess. Many people do not like the game because it is hard to learn and once you learn how to play, the combinations are so numerous that it is impossible to conquer. Some think the game is too boring.

I like that there is no luck involved. Chess cannot be won or lost on the random roll of the dice, or the whim of the wind, or because your equipment breaks, or because the ref missed a foul. It is just one brain versus the other.

I consider chess to be a great equalizer. If I were to play football with a five-year-old, I would knock them into dust, after the ball was snapped, because I have a slight weight advantage. My first tournament in chess was a different story. I was already an adult when this happened. I registered, the match list came out, and I was playing at table nine. I sat down and started setting up the board, as my opponent had not yet shown up. I was ready to go when an eight-year-old boy came and sat down across the table from me. Excuse me, where are this young child's parents? You really should not be sitting here as I have a game to play soon. Oh no! This was my opponent. Are you kidding me? How is this good? If I win, I beat a little kid. If I lose, I lose to a little kid. The game began and it did not take long to realize I was losing. Eventually I lost the game. A quick lesson in humility if there ever was one. Welcome to the game of chess, rookie! My next match was against a fourteen-year-old girl. What is going on? I am stuck in a day of humiliation. I am now proud to say I did not lose to her. We actually tied in what chess rules call a stalemate. Take that, little fourteen-year-old girl.

Each piece in the game of chess has value. Some, like the queen, are considered more valuable because of their ability to move and conquer, whereas some would consider a pawn as being less valuable. Usually you would want to keep the higher valued pieces if you can. Sometimes a person may trade a higher valued piece to get a space or time advantage on the board. This is called a sacrifice. It is one of the most interesting moves in the game. It has the appearance of being an error. It is a thing of beauty when the person doing the sacrifice wins the game.

Chess can also teach us lessons about life. With chess, there is a battle between two opponents. The king rules the side you play on. Nothing else matters except the king. If the king dies, you lose the game.

At this very moment, there is a battle going on between two kings. Both kings are longing for our souls. Our king is either Jesus or Satan, depending on which side you wish to fight. If you say you do not want to be on a side, you automatically choose the side of Satan. You do not have a choice, you have to play the game and choose a king.

Just because you are not the king, it does not mean your life does not have value or that you do not have choices. The move you make is your choice. I might be a knight and, after looking over the board, contemplating a move to either square B5 or D5. That choice is mine to make. In life, you work in a field that fits you best. You choose the direction you want your life to go, but that does not mean you are not serving your king. There are many choices a person can make and still serve their king. The king wants you on his side because you are valuable to him.

For those who choose Jesus, your king is going to ask great things of you. He is going to ask you to do battle. He is going to ask you to fight. He is going to ask you to do things you think are impossible. It will not be easy. He is going to ask you to sacrifice your life. Yeah, you read that right.

It really bugs me when we tell people all they have to do to be saved is to say a prayer and be forgiven, and then we let them go on with their lives as usual. We tend to not act as a mentor or help them grow and mature in faith. It is true that faith and not works save us, but they need to understand the severity of that commitment. I did not marry my wife and then continue my old lifestyle. I did not tell her that I was glad we were married but I was going to continue to date other women. How ridiculous would that be? That is how we treat God sometimes. I love you God, but I love myself more, so I am going to continue to live the way I want. Thank you for saving me, Lord, now how can you help me accomplish my wishes? I am glad we are now in this relationship, but I am not ready to give up my wants completely. When I became a husband I changed my ways because I love my wife and I want to see her happy. I want what she wants more than the things I want. The same thing works with God. If you love him, you will want what he wants more than what you want.

You might ask if we really have to become a sacrifice. Romans 12:1 states, "Therefore, I urge you, brothers and sisters, in view of God's mercy, to offer your bodies as a living sacrifice, holy and pleasing to God—this is your true and proper worship."

One of the definitions of the word "sacrifice" is "destruction or surrender of something for the sake of something else."[1] When I think of the hardest thing Jesus had to do, I used to think of him dying on the cross. Although that would have been very hard, I now think the hardest thing was leaving heaven. Jesus did not have to leave his home in heaven. He did not have to come to Earth. He did not have to die for our sins. He chose to leave heaven and become a sacrifice because he loves us. Romans 5:8 states, "But God demonstrates his own love for us in this: While we were still sinners, Christ died for us." In view of the ultimate sacrifice of Jesus for us, becoming a living sacrifice for him is only "reasonable." Galatians 2:20 states, "I have been crucified with Christ. It is no longer I who live, but Christ who lives in me. And the life I now live in the flesh I live by faith in

---

1. Merriam-Webster, "Sacrifice."

the Son of God, who loved me and gave himself for me." We fight against the enemy, willing to sacrifice ourselves because we love our king and he is more important than our flesh. To follow God means to be crucified with him. This means we give up our lives or sacrifice our lives.

How do we do this? We start to understand with Romans 12:2—"Do not be conformed to this world, but be transformed by the renewal of your mind." How do we define the world? First John 2:15–16 states, "Do not love the world or the things in the world. If anyone loves the world, the love of the Father is not in him. For all that is in the world—the desires of the flesh and the desires of the eyes and pride of life—is not from the Father."

The lust of the flesh includes things that appeal to our physical needs like food, drink, and sex. Lust of the eyes involves possessions like cars, houses, and even other people. The pride of life includes any ambition for that which puffs us up and puts us on the throne of our own lives. These three temptations are interesting to me. In the fourth chapter of Matthew, the devil uses flesh (stone to bread), eyes (you see all these kingdoms), and pride (jump and your God will save you) to tempt Jesus.[2]

What did Jesus do? He kept his focus on what was important and told Satan to take a hike. All too often we get so wrapped up in the things of this world that we forget that we are to transform. Our home is not here, but in heaven—just like the prophets, judges, and disciples of old thought. They had their reservations but still did what the king asked. Moses stood up to Pharaoh. Joshua trusted the Lord against their enemies. Daniel would not bow down. The list goes on. These men were not perfect. They loved God, their king, more than they did their physical lives. I fear we may be more interested in worldly treasure than in telling Satan to take a hike.

When we try to take control of our lives and seek what we want without regard for God, it's like we are taking the place of the king piece on the chessboard. But I have no desire to be the king in real life. I would not do a good job. My life would be a lot worse off if I were king. I am better suited to be another piece in the game. I am much better off allowing Jesus to be my king.

Becoming a sacrifice is not an easy choice. Sometimes it means losing friends, working somewhere else, even losing your family. How can we go through something like this? You have to love your king. This is what he desires. You can only do this if you are truly in love. You have to love him more than your physical self. You have to believe in him with every part of your life. You have to trust him even when it does not make sense.

2. Matt 4:1–11.

Luke 9:23–25 states, "If any man will come after me, let him deny himself, and take up his cross daily, and follow me. For whoever wants to save their life will lose it, but whoever loses their life for me will save it. For what is a man advantaged, if he gain the whole world, and lose himself, or be cast away?"

We should never be afraid to live a sacrificial life. If we have that relationship with our king, he will transform us for service to him. There are five verses where Jesus tells us to take up our cross and follow him. We must forgo our will and seek his. When we do, our relationship grows stronger. In turn, our trust grows to the point that we understand that Jesus has our best interest in mind, and we know he will do what is best for us. I trust in my king to take care of me, even to death.

When I asked Bev to marry me, I knew I was not only changing her life but I was asking for my life to change, from that moment on, forever more. It was a serious step. From experience, I can say there is something special that happens when you find that person you know will be right for you. It is about more than physical attraction. This is a person you intend to see for the rest of your life. It is a huge commitment!

Many times, I do not believe we take it seriously enough. For instance, after Bev and I were engaged, we talked about the future. She was not crazy about flying in airplanes. She had a fear of them and was scared when I would leave to go flying. She knew I wanted to be a pilot. I remember telling her that I hoped she was okay with that because that was where I wanted to go with my life. Did you catch that? I was still worried about my life and my wants. I was saying, I love you but I am still going to do what I want to do.

When you commit to somebody else, your attitude has to change. I knew Bev would never make me change the desires of my life, but I had not fully given myself to her yet. If I had, then I would have been willing to change my career for her. Not that she was asking me to do that, but it was about my heart, my attitude, and my intent. If I was not willing to give myself to her fully, then why was I asking her to commit herself to me? I believe I did have full commitment before we got married but I should have done it sooner.

We call ourselves Christians but do nothing to show our love for God. We might not have committed fully to him yet. I remember sitting in Sunday school one day and I told the group I was unsure if I could leave my high-paying job if I thought God was calling me to be a preacher at a small church with little pay. By the way, I did not feel God was calling me to that job. I remember one of the persons in the group had a funny look on his face. After the service, he came up to me and said, "Confession is good for the soul." My first thought was, I was not confessing, just trying to be honest. Then it hit me. I did need to confess and ask God to forgive me. Why? I was not sacrificing my all to him. How could I be in a relationship if I was not willing to do this?

Full commitment is the place at which we need to arrive. It is only through full commitment that we will find true love. There may be something in your life that is giving you distress. Maybe you feel you cannot fully trust enough. You want to give your all but are afraid.

Committing to Bev was one of the best days of my life. Committing to Jesus was one of the best days of my life. Once you decide to commit your life instead of just existing, the love grows, it matures, and it solidifies. How do you think Bev would have felt if I did not commit to her? I would think she should feel like I could love her more. She probably would have felt I did not love her very much. How do you think Jesus feels when we do not commit to him?

Maybe you think you cannot trust Jesus because it will make your life too hard. Maybe you feel he will not allow you to follow your dreams. Do not be afraid. Jesus will not let you down. He is the only one in whom you can place your full trust. Become that proper and reasonable living sacrifice and show God how much you love him. You will not regret it.

CHAPTER 9

Focusing on Go

(Fulfilling the Great Commission)

IN SOME CULTURES, ARRANGED marriages are normal. An arranged marriage is a type of union in which other individuals join the groom and bride together. Arranged marriages are done for different reasons, including religion, poverty, limited choices, customs, politics, etc. Usually it is the parents of the bride and groom who make the choice. It is an arrangement done more like a business contract. There are a few places where this still exists, but the practice has declined substantially in the last two hundred years.

Besides those annoying human rights issues, there are positives and negatives to arranged marriages. For me it would mean getting past that dating period that I loathe. On the other hand, there is no guarantee of finding love.

Unfortunately, religion seems to work like an arranged marriage for many people. Their parents introduce them to their religion and say this is the best way. When they are young, the children are willing to go along with it because they trust their parents. At some point, as the child grows, they start making their own decisions about what is best for themselves. Once they are an adult, they act upon those decisions.

I have seen three decisions come from arranged relationships with God. Some find themselves unhappy, disenchanted with that relationship. They never fully gave themselves to the relationship. In this case, the person usually falls away from the religion because they are frustrated. They are cold, apathetic unbelievers.

There are some in this arranged marriage who find love. They give themselves and commit to the relationship. These people usually live for their God, starting from a young age. They are typically hot, passionate, hardworking, spiritually active believers. These people will study God and learn his ways. They will take part in their religious services and take ownership. The relationship will last fifty years or more and be looked upon as admirable.

The third is what I call lazy. They continue in their faith but do not understand why. They perform rituals but do not bother to study and learn. They follow blindly, day in and day out, because that is just the way it is. In this case, the love is not strong. It is lukewarm. This is not good, and some churches are full with lukewarm individuals. Imagine being in a marriage where you just live day to day and do not care about each other. There is no love. Each one only looks out for himself or herself. That is not much of a marriage.

Isaiah 29:13 states, "The Lord says: 'These people come near to me with their mouth and honor me with their lips, but their hearts are far from me. Their worship of me is based on merely human rules they have been taught.'" Isaiah was dealing with a problem of apathy. The people were sacrificing and performing the rituals that God had given them, but their hearts were in the wrong place. They were going through the motions without caring. Isaiah said they were like the people of Sodom and Gomorrah. Wow! They were not in a proper relationship.

Revelation 3:15–16 states, "I know your deeds, that you are neither cold nor hot. I wish you were either one or the other! So, because you are lukewarm—neither hot nor cold—I am about to spit you out of my mouth." The people in this type of relationship are not effective. They are just happy existing. They are not growing or leading others to this fantastic experience. They are not only hampering the growth of other people but are missing the greatest relationship ever created.

Most of the time arranged spiritual marriages are the norm when it comes to religion. We might introduce God to others but are lazy in our teaching. As a result, we promote lazy believers. They sit in pews for thirty years, follow rituals, and believe they are doing well. People may believe in God but never experience the fullness that awaits.

This exact same thing is what happened to me in my relationship with Jesus Christ. Raised in the church, my parents introduced me to Jesus. I asked Jesus to save me at seven years old. Now when I say "saved," I mean there was something that drew me to say a sinner's prayer. For me, it was my aunt. She had just died from cancer. I did not fully understand but I knew she was gone. My mind wondered about her eternity. Where was her soul? My parents said she did not believe in Jesus. My parents did not raise me to be scared but I think I said this sinner's prayer because I was scared about going to hell someday.

This also did not mean I had a relationship with Jesus. I might have been going to church every Sunday, but that does not mean my heart transformed. It would be nice if everybody that believed actually loved Jesus with *all* of their heart, but it does not always work this way. I actually failed to go to church for a couple of years after high school. I was working and the business scheduled me to work on Sundays. It was a convenient excuse to stay out of church. I was not praying. This means I was not talking to Jesus. I was not reading the Bible. This means I was not listening to Jesus. I did not feel I was necessarily doing anything bad but I now look back on it as an apathetic relationship. Just being good does not matter if we are not walking with Jesus. I convinced myself that I was too busy. It is true that I was very busy during this time. I was working forty hours a week and going to school at the same time. Again, it was a convenient excuse. What kind of relationship is it when you never talk to each other? It is not one. There should be no excuses that come between you and Jesus. What had happened was that I had found the love of Jesus, but I had not found my love for Jesus.

Bev and I actually grew up in the same church, from a very early age. We did not know each other that well but we did know each other. Neither one of us thought about dating the other person while we were growing up. After high school, we went our separate ways. I moved away and she was doing her thing. I did not see her at all for a couple of years. Eventually, we ended up coming back to the same place and attending the same church again.

This time something was different. I remember one Sunday sitting in the pew and thinking about her in a way that I had not in the past. There was an attraction that was present that I did not see before. I started wondering if she would be interested in dating and if she would be a good fit for a relationship.

One day after all of those years of saying I was a Christian and not having a relationship with Jesus, I saw something different. I was reading, listening, studying, praying, and I saw Jesus in a different way. My mind switched and I saw somebody I wanted to get to know better. This was somebody with whom I wanted to grow closer. Just as it happened with Bev, it happened with Jesus. He was there the whole time, waiting patiently for me to find the proper love relationship. It took a while to see but he was there the entire time. Finding the love I had for Jesus made me want to do things for him. Instead of just receiving, I wanted to give.

After the resurrection of Jesus, he was speaking to the disciples and was preparing to leave them to sit at the right hand of God. The disciples were wondering about the next steps, so Jesus gave them a command. Jesus did not say to go and sit on the bank and wait for him to return. Matthew 28:19 states, "Go ye therefore, and teach all nations, baptizing them in the name of the Father, and of the Son, and of the Holy Ghost." Go! Get to moving! We call this the Great Commission. There are hundreds of places in the Bible in which God instructs his people to go. It is not just for the disciples. It is for us also.

If we have fallen in love with Jesus and have entered into a covenant relationship with him, we should want to do what he wants. He wants us to go teach. He wants us to go show others the way.

Unfortunately, too many Christians would rather sit in a pew for thirty years. They want to be fed by the Peters of the world. The great commission is not just for the apostles. It is not just for pastors, evangelists, missionaries, prophets, and teachers. The Great Commission is for every believer. Jesus said, "The harvest is plentiful but the workers are few."[1] Jesus wants us to be disciples, but the command is not to stay still. The command is to go!

Going does not necessarily mean to transfer to a different part of the world. Then again, it might mean we relocate. I think we often miss that point. As a result, we end up doing nothing. Going means to reach out to the lost, wherever they may be located. Guess what. They are located right where I am currently living. We are not all meant to be pastors, teachers, or deacons, but that does not mean we sit still. We should be leading them to Christ. We serve a God who wants us to go.

One reason people give for not leading a ministry is they fear they will fail. I have taught in various settings for over twenty-five years. I always fear I am going to do terribly as I am leading a ministry. About two years ago, I had some time on my hands and thought I would start a new ministry. I love to play the game of chess, so I decided to start a Christian chess club. On the first night, we had three people show up, including myself. What

1. Matt 9:37.

I did not consider is that a ministry should involve fellowship. When you are playing chess, you usually do not talk. You sit and are quiet. I had not thought that one all the way through. It went downhill from there. Turns out people around me did not like chess as much as I did.

When I think about failing, I think about that chess club. By the world's standard, that effort would be considered a failure. God's standard is not our standard. The world tends to measure our success by the number of people involved. God is not interested in your ability to reach grandness. He just wants you to go. Ephesians 2:10 states, "For we are God's handiwork, created in Christ Jesus to do good works, which God prepared in advance for us to do." He did not say you have to do something big. He just says you are to do good. Doing a work for the right reason is creating grandness. God can take something small but good and make something great out of it. We may never even see those great results ourselves, but do not doubt what God is doing with your work. God looks at your heart. Even though the chess club no longer exists, I think of that ministry as a success. God knows I was trying to love others through this activity. Do not be afraid of mistakes. Learn from mistakes and do your ministry for the right reason. You will not fail.

Some people are introverted and do not feel they can lead a ministry. I consider myself extremely introverted. I used to have people tell me they thought I was stuck up. Then, once they got to know me, they thought I had a great personality. When you fear leading, it is really Satan telling you that you cannot do it. Do not believe it. It is a lie. I have had to force myself into leading ministries but it has paid off so much for me.

You may also have to force yourself into acting. Satan has ways of stopping your ministry. I cannot tell you how many times I told myself I was being silly, thinking I could write a book. Eventually, I reached the thought that I may fail at writing but it is not going to be because I quit. Publishers may say I am a terrible writer. Readers may put me down. None of that can stop me from trying my best and following through with spreading the word of God.

A ministry does not have to be overly complex. We have a person in our church who puts together packages during the holidays and takes them over to the older people in the nursing home. This is a great service. She gets volunteers to prepare the packages and go with her to the home. They receive a blessing from this activity and the older folks get to see Jesus at work.

Some people are afraid they will mess up the gospel message. They feel that if they mess it up, they will ruin a person's life. If you really believe there is a literal place called hell, where people will suffer for eternity, how much are you going to mess them up by telling them about Christ? You cannot make their soul fall into a worse situation.

Maybe you think you cannot find your place. You are not a teacher, preacher, etc. There are so many ways to take the lead. There are literally hundreds of things you can do. You can start researching online by looking up various ways to minister, disciple, and lead people to Jesus.

If it comes down to the fact that you just do not know what to do, then reach out to your pastor. Tell him you are interested in starting a ministry but do not know what to do. I suggest evaluating your likes and dislikes, your strengths and weaknesses, and finding something that fits.

I like reading Christian books in my spare time. I thought there must be others who enjoy reading these books also. Therefore, I started a Christian book club. Sharing theological truths with others is much better than doing life alone. The club has been going for over three years. It was actually the book club that inspired me to write this book. Writing a book is a new ministry I have undertaken. There are so many options.

For those who just do not feel confident in doing ministry, do you feel anxious? Do you feel like God would like more from you? That is because God has designed us to move and you are not using your mind and body for that for which it was designed. You are not fulfilling the purpose of the designer. It is the enemy keeping you from your design.

Let me give an example. My wife has hummingbird feeders on our back patio. Hummingbirds are fun to watch. Sometimes I like to sit in my chair, put my feet up, listen to some Christian music, and watch the hummingbirds. In those moments, I am relaxed, calm, and thoughtful.

We used to live in Fort Worth, Texas. I lived about twelve miles from my place of work. Sometimes it took me close to an hour to get home from work. Why? The enemy was keeping me from moving. The enemy in this case was the other cars, because it was bumper to bumper, ten miles per hour, and at times stopped. In those moments, I was aggravated, stressed, and wanted to stop being a Christian.

During the time in the car, I was still sitting, listening to Christian music, and looking at birds out of the window. So, what is the difference? Home is a place designed for relaxing. When I am relaxing at home, I am fulfilling its designed purpose. The interstate is a place designed to move.

When I am stressed in the car, I am not fulfilling its designed purpose. If all of those other drivers were not on the interstate, I could go fast and not be stressed. Even though I am doing the same things in both scenarios, one is good and the other is bad.

God designed us to go. If we do not go, the family of God does not grow. If we do not go, we are not really loving our neighbor. I think of the story of Jonah. He ran when God told him to go. He would have rather died than to see those people saved. How can we love our neighbor and want to see them go to hell?

When we fight against that design to go, we are going to be frustrated. We are going to be stressed. We are going to be anxious. I am positive there are current ministries in which you can participate. It is not an option. Follow God by doing what he designed you to do. Get to moving and lead others to Christ.

CHAPTER 10

Heroes among Us

(Loving Others by Going to Church)

WHEN I WAS IN my twenties, the future looked bright. I was finished with college, I was newly married, and we had just bought our first home. We were living in Salem, Illinois. It is a small town with a population of about seven thousand. We were attending a small church that ran close to one hundred people every Sunday.

There was a woman who had been coming to our church by herself but had not been there in the last three weeks. One of the members of the church, Don Donoho, and I went out visiting and thought we would stop by her house. Not only did we not make it into the house, we did not even make it to the front door. Her husband, who was huge, met us on the lawn by the curb with an attitude of authority, telling us we needed to leave. His attitude toward Christians was clear. We told him we were just wondering how his wife was doing and if she needed anything. He said no and that all was well.

Don then took a moment to invite the man to church on Sunday. His excuse for not going was that Sundays were his day to ride horses and drink beer. Okay, at least he was honest.

I began turning to go to the car when I heard Don say something I will never forget. He said, "Well, Jesus drank wine and rode on a donkey, and that did not keep him out of church!" Whoa! With this man's attitude and size, I did not know what to think next. Were we going to have to make a run for safety? I did not know if I could outrun him but I knew I could outrun Don, so all was good. I turned back around and the man was speechless. He did not know what to say to that. It actually calmed him down, but after a few seconds, he repeated that we should leave and we did.

Why should we belong to a church? I cannot tell you how many times I have heard people say they have stopped going because they are tired of the traditional church environment. They come up with many excuses for not attending. Some of these excuses are better than drinking beer and riding horses. Some of them are not. We need to examine God's word to see if attendance is important or not. I cannot imagine our attendance record sitting in heaven waiting for us.

First, we should define church. Webster's dictionary defines it as a building used for public worship.[1] In the Bible, the word comes from the Greek word *ecclesia*. Whenever used, ecclesia refers to people. In John chapter 3, verse 5, Jesus is teaching the Pharisee Nicodemus. He tells Nicodemus he must be born again. "No one can see the kingdom of God unless they are born again."[2] Nicodemus had a hard time understanding the meaning of this. According to Galatians 3:26–29, when a person trusts Jesus as their savior, they are born again. This means they become a new person, neither Jew nor gentile. We happen to call them Christians, and all Christians make up the church.

The New Testament brings up imagery to help us understand. It uses metaphors such as the church is the body of Christ and Jesus is the head.[3] The church is the people of God. The church is the Bride of Christ. There is no doubt that born again Christians are the church. The church is not some building in which we meet. People are the church. As such, we can meet with Jesus anywhere. The building we go to has no special powers. So, do we have to get together?

Why should we belong to a church? I was talking to somebody else who said they had been going to church for about thirty years and could not remember the sermons, so what was the point in continuing to go to church? First, I thought that was sad. I hope that we are learning and growing in our Christian faith. I responded with this: "I have eaten for thirty years. I do not remember what I had to eat six days ago, but I am sure it nourished my body. If I had not eaten for thirty years, I would be dead. In the same way, church nourishes your soul. If you had not been there you would be spiritually dead. You just do not realize you are being nourished."

1. Merriam-Webster, "Church."
2. John 3:5.
3. Col 1:18.

The man said he could watch sermons on television or YouTube to receive nourishment. That is true, and I think it is a good idea to listen to other evangelists and teachers outside the church building.

Why should we belong to a church? So far, we have run across some flimsy excuses and there are many more out there. Just about every excuse we make falls apart. I had a man tell me they did not need to go to church to be a Christian. It is true that we can meet with Christ anywhere we are located, but what does God think? Does the Bible say anything about going to church? We want to make sure we are meeting with God. Matthew 18:20 states, "For where two or three are gathered in my name, there am I among them." This does not mean a building called a church as Webster defines it, but it does mean getting together with other believers. The first-century believers would have met in homes and other various places. As such, you become a community of believers, helping each other. We all need help with our faith. If you are not going to a church building, where are you doing this?

Hebrews 10:25 states, "Not neglecting to meet together, as is the habit of some, but encouraging one another, and all the more as you see the day drawing near." Not meeting together is not a new problem. This is a direct command to meet together and even calls out the people who have said they do not have to do so.

Romans 1:11–12 states, "I long to see you so that I may impart to you some spiritual gift to make you strong—that is, that you and I may be mutually encouraged by each other's faith." Paul had a desire to impart a spiritual gift to help them. He also thought he would be encouraged by meeting with them. We meet with other Christians because we encourage each other. As humans, we are not perfect. We are bombarded with deceptions. We fail all of the time. In church, we lift each other up. In church, we listen to each other's problems and weep with others in times of trouble. In church, we rejoice in the good times. In church, we become a community that loves each other. In church, we make each other stronger. In church, we help each other get through life.

There is no getting around it. We are to meet with other Christians. We lift each other up, and that means giving of your time and effort for the sake of others. That does not have to be in a building we call church, but we cannot do it on our own. Belonging to a church means being a part of a community. We are commanded to meet.

Just because this is a command does not mean it is a chore. This should not be something we hate to do. Belonging to a church is something we enjoy as an outpouring of our love for God's people.

In 1 Corinthians 12, Paul talks about us being the body of Christ and that there is only one body but there are many parts of the body. He uses this analogy to describe the church. We have each been given spiritual gifts to be used for God and the church. The analogy compares our gifts with body parts to show how we would be handicapped without that part or gift. Think about your body. If you did not have a leg, life would be harder. If you have a spiritual gift that others do not have and keep it to yourself, then church is harder for the others. Every part is special in its own way. Personally, I think a person is selfish if they are not willing to share their gift with the rest of the body.

Why should we belong to a church? I had a man tell me they did not like going to church anymore because they felt the church was full of hypocrites. I think there are probably some hypocrites in the church. There are also hypocrites at the local Walmart. That does not keep you from shopping there. The Bible is clear that we are to meet together. If you are not meeting with other believers, then you are not doing what Jesus wants us to do. I think calling yourself a Christian and not meeting with other Christians makes you a hypocrite. Do you think you are better than everybody else is? Zig Ziglar said, "If a hypocrite is standing between you and God, it just means the hypocrite is closer to God than you are."[4]

I once asked a group of people why they went to church. The answers were to worship God, to receive a blessing, to learn, etc. These are all good answers, but I was bothered. Every answer was a selfish reason. I asked why nobody answered that they went to give to and serve others. Pastor Travis Penn taught me this a long time ago. How would I learn if somebody was not teaching? How would I receive a blessing if nobody gave that to me? How would I worship God if there were not people playing music? I, I, I, I, I. When did the church become about me? How about getting up on Sunday morning with the attitude of serving others? What can I do today to help somebody else in his or her walk with Christ? By having a purpose in attending, church becomes much more exciting and desirable. I wake up wanting to go instead of it being a chore I have to survive.

I have heard people say that church is outdated. The music is not good and the preaching is either boring or judgmental. Outside of the church,

4. Ziglar, *Confessions of a Happy Christian*, 146.

we are inundated with consumer advertisements. Businesses cater to our every whim because they are trying to sell us something. As a result, we can shop around to get what we want. It is about pleasing us. The problem is that when we live in a consumer world, we cannot seem to turn it off come church time. I like the music at church B better than at church A. I like the preaching at church C better than at church B. Many churches have fallen prey to this type of thought and have special events with the purpose of filling the pews. They might even water down the gospel message to please the crowd. They probably have good intentions of saving souls, but the consumer sees it differently. The consumer is looking for what pleases them. We need an attitude of pleasing others. We have to be very careful that the church does not become just a business, attempting to fill empty seats.

When you meet with others, you may sometimes wonder what you are getting out of it. It may seem boring or useless at times. What you are really doing during those times is meeting with real people who have real needs. We all have good times and bad times in our lives. Meeting with others who become our friends helps us to get through the bad and rejoice in the good. There is hope in the church. There is joy in the church. We are not perfect. We are all just sinners who have been saved by grace. Through those meetings, we find real faith and we mature in Christ.

Looking back to my childhood church, I no longer see them as normal people. I think of the people who taught me about Jesus. I think of Bill and Claudette Merriman, who taught Sunday school classes and helped with singing. I think of Lee and Kay Penn, who taught our junior church and played the music. I think of Micky and Barb Russell, who taught our Sunday school classes. I think of John and Marsha Merold, who taught the little kids in children's church. I think of my parents for teaching me. I think of Wallace Malone, who was our preacher and spent countless hours mentoring, and his wife, Eunice, who taught Sunday school. I think of Ivan and Nila Maxwell and Mike and Donna Stevenson, who led the youth groups. I think of Marilyn Drabing, who knelt at an old-fashioned alter and prayed with me when I asked Jesus into my heart. The names of the people that come to mind could take up an entire book in itself.

These people were willing to share their time and effort with me. Not because they received money. Not because they received praise or reward. They did it because they cared about me. They loved me. Did you catch that? They loved me. I did not understand that until later in life. We might get something out of going to church, but that is not the purpose of church.

Loving God and loving others is the real reason we belong to a church. We love Jesus, so we keep his commands. We understand what the love of Jesus has done in our lives and want other people to experience that love. Therefore, we share. These people were not Jew or gentile. They were not just normal people. They were special. They were born again Christians. They were my heroes.

CHAPTER 11

Forgiveness

(Just How Important Is It?)

LIFE IS DANGEROUS. GROWING up, I encountered several physical issues. I have had two surgeries, a broken leg, two appendages needing stitches, and numerous minor injuries. It is a wonder we live so long. Most of that physical pain came at the hands of myself. I was the one who wrecked my bike. I was the one who twisted my ankle.

Some people go through extreme pain. As much physical pain as I have experienced, the strongest I have encountered has come from the hands of other people. It comes in the form of emotional pain. Other people being abusive toward you can create some of the strongest pain you will ever encounter. Unfortunately, the people who will hurt you the most are the ones you love the most. That is because we trust them. We believe they are on our side and will not hurt us. We have unrealistic expectations, but, at some point, the pain will come.

How do you handle those situations? Some people get mad easily. The littlest things set them off. They are quick to jump on the offender, sometimes creating a large, screaming argument. I, personally, am the opposite way. I tend to get offended and keep it in. I like keeping the peace. Oftentimes, the other person does not even know I was offended. All that does is build anger within.

Sometimes the offense is small, like somebody gossiping about you or not paying you what they owe you. Sometimes the offense is big, like sexual assault or murder.

When I was a young pilot, I had thoughts of becoming a missionary pilot. One missionary pilot, named Nate Saint, flew himself and four other missionaries into the jungle of Ecuador to reach an Indian tribe. Nate and Marjorie had a son named Steve. Steve was five years old when Mincaye, an Indian tribesman, murdered his father. It was because of that experience that others were able to reach the tribe. Steve went back to the United States and became successful in his career. Then he went back to the jungle. That experience led him to forgive the person who had killed his dad. They actually became lifelong friends. Steve wrote a book, which also became a movie, entitled *The End of the Spear*.[1]

Steve's life changed forever. He had a new normal. After losing his father, how could Steve possibly forgive the killer? Forgiving is one of the hardest things to do and is part of the reason people struggle with Christianity. People struggle to make sense of forgiveness without vengeance. Let us try to give it some meaning.

Some people like holding on to bitterness. They will tell you they do not, but they cannot get rid of it. By holding on to our anger toward a person, it somehow feels like justice is accomplished. It is like saying, "You did me wrong, and you deserve my wrath. If I do not stay angry, then I will be letting you off the hook." The issue is that mental problems are harder to deal with than physical problems.

Imagine if somebody took a knife and cut you. Would you just let that open wound fester? No, you would not! You would go to the hospital and have the doctor stitch it up. We have to fix that wound before it becomes infected. Mentally hurting us does the same thing, but for some reason we let it fester instead of getting it taken care of. The longer we hold on to it, the higher the chance of becoming infected. Infected means anger and bitterness, not only against the offender, but also in other areas of our lives. We have to find a way to get rid of it.

We might have a misunderstanding of what it means to forgive. When you forgive somebody, it does not mean you now condone his or her behavior. Just because Steve Saint forgave Mincaye, it did not mean he agreed with the killing. A person who murders still deserves punishment under the law. If somebody was sexually assaulting you, that still needs to stop and justice needs to happen. You cannot let it continue to happen.

When you forgive somebody, it does not mean your pain will go away. I have to imagine Steve Saint still missed his father. I lost my mother

---

1. Saint, *End of the Spear*.

when I was twenty-nine years old. There are times I still hurt. There is a process of handling grief. It may take time. Do not fall under a misconception that you have to feel good before you can forgive. You may still be grieving your situation.

When you forgive somebody, it does not mean you will be friends again. Romans 12:18 states, "If it is possible, as far as it depends on you, live at peace with everyone." If possible, it is good to be reconciled, but you cannot control the thoughts of the other person. They might not care. They may have no desire to be your friend. When Jesus was dying on the cross, he said, "Father forgive them."[2] There are people who do not wish to be reconciled with God.

You also are not required to trust that person. If a person has cheated you many times, and you feel you cannot trust them, you have no obligation to continue in the same relationship. Proverbs 26:11 states, "As a dog returns to its vomit, so fools repeat their folly." You do not have to be a forgiving fool. A part of the forgiving process is for the person who was offended. When we forgive, we are doing ourselves a favor. Why should we be miserable when the other person does not even care?

Besides psychology, does God have anything to say about forgiveness? Matthew 18:21–35 gives us a story between Jesus and Peter that is perfect for understanding what God desires of us. In verse 21 Peter states, "Lord, how many times shall I forgive my brother or sister who sins against me? Up to seven times?"[3] As we read about Peter, we get this glimpse of a person that wears his emotions on his sleeve. He is the first to jump from the boat. He is the first to the tomb. He is the one who uses the sword. Often, Peter gets himself into trouble because of his compulsiveness. I get an idea that Peter is speaking about a particular, unnamed person. Maybe this person had done him wrong six or seven times and Peter is ready to let this person go. Before he does, he thought he'd better check with Jesus.

In verse 22 Jesus says, "I tell you, not seven times, but seventy-seven times."[4] Jesus is not stating an amount. He is saying we need to forgive people an unlimited amount of times. Think about how many times you have committed offense against God. Then think about how many times God has forgiven you. My guess is much more than seven.

2. Luke 23:34.

3. Matt 18:21.

4. Matt 18:22.

He could have just left it there, but Peter probably would have gone away disappointed. Jesus decided to give him a parable.

Starting in verse 23 Jesus says, "Therefore, the kingdom of heaven is like a king who wanted to settle accounts with his servants."[5] God is the king and we are the servants. Romans 6:20 states, "When you were slaves to sin, you were free from the control of righteousness."

The story continues in verse 24. They brought a servant to the king who owed him ten thousand bags of gold. There was no way this servant was going to be able to pay what he owed. This is similar to our sins. We have sin debt that we cannot pay. We will never have enough money.

Verse 25 states, "Since he was not able to pay, the master ordered that he and his wife and his children and all that he had be sold to repay the debt."[6] This is the idea of separation. You can call it hell. You can call it something else, but it is a separation from God and is undesirable.

Verse 26 says that the servant fell on his knees and begged the king. He said, "Be patient with me, and I will pay back everything."[7] This is the view we get when we come to Jesus. We have our sin debt and we cannot fix it on our own. What can we do? We beg Jesus for help.

Verse 27 states, "The servant's master took pity on him, canceled the debt and let him go."[8] Hallelujah! This is one of my favorite verses in the Bible. When I could not find a way, Jesus found it for me. When I could not do it on my own, Jesus did it for me. By dying on the cross, Jesus paid that debt when I could not. We just have to reach out and receive that forgiveness.

It would be good enough to stop the story there, but Jesus helps Peter a little further. Verse 28 says that servant then went out and found one of his fellow servants, who owed him a hundred silver coins. Now Jesus turns from talking about the God/man relationship and talks about the man/man relationship. The hundred silver coins is obviously less than the ten thousand bags of gold the first man owed the king. This represents the idea that the sins of man are so much greater against God than any offense toward men.

The first man grabbed his fellow servant and began to choke him, demanding to be paid for what the person owed him. The fellow servant had no way of paying back what he owed. So, what did he do? He did the same

5. Matt 18:23.

6. Matt 18:25.

7. Matt 18:26.

8. Matt 18:27.

thing as the first man. He fell to his knees and begged him to be patient and he will pay it back.

This time was different. This man is begging for mercy but the first man throws him in prison until he could pay the debt. Since he will never be able to pay the debt, it is a life sentence. He will be in prison forever. It is scary to consider, but hell is forever.

The other servants were outraged. In verse 31, they go and tell the master what is going on. The master calls the first man back in and chastises him. Verse 32 states, "'You wicked servant, I canceled all that debt of yours because you begged me to. Shouldn't you have had mercy on your fellow servant just as I had on you?' In anger his master handed him over to the jailers to be tortured, until he should pay back all he owed."[9] Matthew 7:2 states, "For in the same way you judge others, you will be judged, and with the measure you use, it will be measured to you."[10] Remember, the first person could never pay back the debt either. Now he was going to be tortured forever. Forever. Forever. Forever. Did I mention forever?

He finishes the parable in verse 35 saying, "This is how my heavenly Father will treat each of you unless you forgive your brother or sister from your heart."[11] Whoa! What? Have you ever played the game *Sorry!*? You knock another player's piece off the board and say, "Sorry." I do not think you are truly sorry it that situation. Notice Jesus is not asking us to give lip service. Saying sorry yet not meaning it does not work. It has to come from the heart.

Matthew 6:14–15 states, "For if you forgive other people when they sin against you, your heavenly Father will also forgive you. But if you do not forgive others their sins, your Father will not forgive your sins." Whoa! What?

Ephesians 4:31–32 states, "Let all bitterness and wrath and anger and clamor and slander be put away from you, along with all malice. Be kind to one another, tender-hearted, forgiving each other, just as God in Christ also has forgiven you."

Hebrews 12:15 states, "See to it that no one comes short of the grace of God; that no root of bitterness springing up causes trouble, and by it many be defiled." Whoa! What? Short of the Grace of God. Bitterness and anger can be considered a sin. God gave us qualities like anger so we could be mad at sin, not at each other. When we get mad at others, we are letting

9. Matt 18:32.

10. Matt 7:2.

11. Matt 18:35.

those qualities cause us harm. We are not following the commandments Jesus said were the greatest—to love God with all your heart and love your neighbor as yourself.[12] Would you not want forgiveness? If we cannot forgive, we are essentially saying we do not appreciate what God has done for us. If you cannot forgive when somebody does you wrong, then how can you expect your father to forgive you?

We could actually miss having a relationship with Jesus, or cause others to miss that relationship. Unless we let go of that anger, we will never experience healing and freedom. We will remain slaves. This forgiveness business is critical in the eyes of God. God views us all as his children and wishes to have a relationship with each one of us.

Recognize that it does not matter how bad you have been. I watched a documentary on the life of mass murderer and cannibal Jeffrey Dahmer. He supposedly turned to Christ before he died. I cannot judge his heart, meaning I cannot say if he is in heaven, but from what I heard him say, I am actually expecting to find him in heaven someday. That may hurt some people. The family members who lost loved ones because of him. Are they going to be able to forgive Jeffrey Dahmer? They probably feel he does not deserve heaven. Remember, none of us deserves heaven. It is a gift. A gift is freely given. There is nothing you have done that Jesus cannot cover.

As a Christian, we are image bearers of Christ. We try to follow his example. He forgave us when we could not pay back our debt. We should treat people better than they deserve. How? You can only do this by increasing your faith in God. Instead of filling your life with junk, fill it with the Holy Spirit and the fruits of the Spirit.

Matthew 5:44 states, "But I tell you, love your enemies and pray for those who persecute you." Have you ever really done that? I am not talking about asking God to curse somebody. I am talking about asking God to bless them. I am talking about asking God to change their hearts and lives. If you are praying for them, you should not be able to stay mad at them for very long. We can also pray for God to help us release forgiveness.

Notice, this is the only chapter in which I did not provide a personal example for correlation. That is because forgiveness is super personal. I have no business telling the world about those who have done me wrong. I do not mind telling the world what I have done wrong, but I have no business telling the world about who I have wronged. That information is only between us. To treat it otherwise would not be treating the other person properly.

12. Matt 22:36–40.

As hard as it can be to forgive somebody for the wrongs they have done to you, something even harder is to forgive yourself. I know it is for me. I have done plenty of stupid things in my life and I have hurt people. I never mean to, but stuff happens anyways. The guilt drives me crazy. It sticks with me for a very long time. I wish a scientist could erase that part of my memory because it hurts, but we need those experiences in our memory.

Understanding your flaws turned you into the person you are now, and not who you used to be. If I had never made a mistake, or recognized the mistake, I would not have found Jesus.

We also need to remember who we are. We may struggle with regrets, but we are children of God. God gives us so much value. He created us in his image. He loves us so much that he wants to be in a relationship with us. Jeremiah Braudrick, in *Removing the Dragon Skin*, states, "When we do not love and value ourselves, we are in essence disagreeing with the Creator that does."[13]

I still consider myself a good person. Not because I am good, but because of what the Lord has done within me. If God can forgive the chief of sinners, I should be able to forgive myself. It hurts me when I hurt others, but I think it is important to understand that the hurt leads us to God.

Anytime you think somebody does not deserve forgiveness, you have to look no further than yourself to find the answer. You do not deserve forgiveness for the things you have done. Daniel 9:9 states, "The Lord our God is merciful and forgiving, even though we have rebelled against him."

We have to realize offense is the work of Satan. He would love nothing more than for us to hold hate in our heart and let it divide us. Satan would love me to think I am too bad for God's forgiveness. Offense is one of the most powerful tools the devil has at his disposal. He wants you to hold on to past strife. Holding on to past hurt means less of God in your heart. It is not the person, but the deception. We should not be mad at the person doing wrong but be mad at the deceiver. Knowing this should help you put your anger in the proper place.

Do not let the devil control you with anger. Do not let another's offense send you to hell. Do not hate the sinner. Hate the sin. Be angry with the great deceiver, and love your neighbor.

13. Braudrick, *Removing the Dragon Skin*, 4.

CHAPTER 12

Preventing Crashes

(Good Communication Builds Great Relationships)

As a pilot, and flight instructor, it is vital to learn from mistakes made in the past. By doing so, we can avoid repeating those mistakes. One accident we studied stood out as particularly silly for communication error.

The Flying Tigers was a scheduled cargo carrier, later bought by FedEx. In 1989, one of their Boeing 747s crashed while attempting to land in Kuala Lumpur. Air Traffic Control (ATC) cleared the aircraft to descend. The terminology used was "Tiger 66, descend two four zero zero," which is 2,400 feet. The pilot misunderstood, thinking the clearance was "descend to four zero zero." Did you catch the subtle difference? There is a difference between the word "two" and "to," but they sound similar on the radio. The pilot radioed back, "Okay, four zero zero," which is 400 feet, and ATC did not catch it. They flew 2,000 feet lower than they should have and hit the hillside at 437 feet.[1] Lives changed forever, all because of a small communication error.

There are hundreds of aviation accidents and incidents we can study. Many are the result of communication error. I see communication errors happening in relationships as well. In my marriage, it happens more now that I am older because my hearing is not as good as it used to be. When we hear things the wrong way, or something is not spoken correctly to us, it can create problems for us. Your spouse may get mad at you. You may not accomplish a very important task. You might spend a lot of time working on a project, just to learn it is not necessary or important. Communication

1. Aviation Safety Network, "Flying Tiger Line 66."

error is very common; to have a healthy relationship we need to work on good communication. This does not apply only to our earthly family; good communication with God is very important as well.

One of the first things to do to create good communication is active listening. The way we do this is to read the Bible. It does very little for us if all we do is listen to the pastor speak a few verses on Sunday morning and not listen to God the rest of the week. We have to take more of an active role in listening. I advise reading other material as well as the Bible. Obviously, since I am trying to sell a book.

I actually read quite a bit, but I do run across a problem from time to time. Active listening goes beyond just hearing the words somebody else is speaking or reading words of the English language. It is important to meditate on what you are reading and hearing. If I am not careful, I can read or listen and have no idea what I just read or heard. What good is that? That is not good communication through active listening.

You also have to think about the context of the words read or spoken. What sort of emotions were taking place? What was going on around them at the time? Why is the other person saying these words to begin with?

One of the biggest hindrances to active listening is forming opinions before understanding the context. Let me give an example. Leviticus 19:28 states, "Do not cut your bodies for the dead or put tattoo marks on your-selves. I am the LORD." At first glance, a person could use this verse, out of context, and simply state it is a sin to get a tattoo. When I do this, I am listening to the word of God but not actively listening. I might be a person who thinks getting a tattoo is a terrible idea, and so I might be biased. As such, I come to this conclusion quickly. It is clear. God said do not do it. Case closed.

When I actively listen, I view the verse in its entire context and listen to why the words are being communicated. What emotions are taking place? I take time to read surrounding verses and meditate on what is happening. When God was speaking to the Israelites, they had just left Egypt and were now between Egypt and Canaan. Archeological evidence has shown that these two societies had rituals concerning markings and cuttings, which they were doing to honor their gods. The Israelites had picked up some of these habits. God is speaking about people following good luck rituals, maybe leaving nothing to chance and looking to other gods as well, instead of just trusting in him. We do the same thing. We trust God until something bad happens in our lives. Then we start reaching out to other sources because we want answers. We want answers now. We are not satisfied with just letting God have control. We might start looking to other sources besides God.

So is it okay for a Christian to get a tattoo? It is not that easy of a question. First Corinthians 10:31 states, "So whether you eat or drink or whatever you do, do it all for the glory of God." A better question to ask would be why would you want the tattoo? Notice the end of God's command. He says, "I am the Lord." The Israelites were looking to other gods. Do you want this tattoo in order to worship other gods? Do you just want to be artistic? Are you trying to make a statement? What would that statement be? Do you want to slam somebody else with your mean thoughts? Do you want to make a political statement? Do you want to show kindness to others? Do you want to print a Bible verse on your hands so that it will constantly be a remembrance? What is your purpose? Once you find your purpose, then you will be actively listening.

Listening is just half of the art of good communication. Speaking effectively greatly improves the chances of success as well. United Airlines Flight 173 is another example of a crash caused by communication error. In 1978, the pilot of the Boeing 707 was attempting to land at Portland, Oregon. There was a malfunction with one of the gear indications. They went into a holding pattern for an hour to solve the mystery. Fuel status was not communicated properly to the captain. It was communicated but not with a sense of urgency. The captain did not interpret the facts with a sense of urgency. If the flight engineer would have communicated differently and maybe said they have so many minutes left instead of just the amount of fuel remaining, then the captain might have done things differently. That is just a guess as we only have one result, but is logical. They ran out of fuel before they could land the aircraft and crashed short of the airport.[2] How you speak can have an effect on how others view the situation.

If we are driving down the road and my wife says "car," my first thought would be to wonder which car she wanted me to see. If she braces her body for an impact and yells "car," my thoughts would turn to what I was about to hit and did not see. My reaction could mean the difference between a crash or not. Therefore, her speech could mean the difference between a crash or not.

Prayer is a fancy word we use for speaking with God. Again, to have a good relationship, we want our communication to be good. How we talk

---

2. National Transportation Safety Board, "United Airlines 173," 27.

to God can greatly improve our relationship. How then should we do this? We could improvise and guess, or we could follow the example provided us. Jesus taught us how to pray. We call it the Lord's Prayer. We find the Lord's Prayer in Matt 6:9–13. There is so much found in those few verses that we could write an entire book on just the Lord's Prayer. For our purpose, we will keep it simple.

When I think of first learning how to pray, I think of when I was a kid. We would say a prayer before we ate a meal. This is a way of saying thank you. I appreciate God supplying my needs for the day. Food is necessary to sustain life. King David said, "The Earth is the Lord's, and everything in it."[3] Our lives are sustained by God Almighty, and we should be thankful for what he has given to us.

Matthew 6:11 states, "Give us today our daily bread." This would not only apply to eating, but we are asking God to take care of all our needs. We must have an understanding that the Lord will take care of our needs. Philippians 4:19 states, "And my God will meet all your needs according to the riches of his glory in Christ Jesus."

Notice we are praying on a daily basis. When we pray, we need to be mindful of what we are asking God. We are not praying for wealth. We are not praying for God to help us with the game. We are praying for him to take care of our needs. Why should we ask this? It is so that we can accomplish his will. It is important to remember why. It is about his will being done. Proverbs 30:8–9 states, "Keep falsehood and lies far from me; give me neither poverty nor riches, but give me only my daily bread. Otherwise, I may have too much and disown you and say, 'Who is the Lord?' Or I may become poor and steal and so dishonor the name of my God."

We often fall into a trap. I am not saying we should not be saving for our futures. I think there is a biblical argument for taking care of our family and the family's future. I am saying God can take care of all our needs. Too much or too little can distract us from God, which would be a tragedy. We pray for our needs so we keep in mind the will of God. Notice where the focus is located. It is not on us, but God.

As we start to understand that we are sinners, then we need to view prayer in a second way. Matthew 6:12 states, "And forgive us our debts, as we also have forgiven our debtors." Sin is our debts. As a sinner, I have broken the law and there has to be reparations for those wrong doings. The problem is that we cannot afford to pay that debt. Nobody can afford to pay

3. Ps 24:1.

that debt. It takes perfection. Only Jesus can pay that debt. We do not deserve it. It is given to us freely. As such, what right do we have to hold other people's debts over their heads? If somebody does us wrong, it is important to forgive, just as God has forgiven us. Notice where the focus is located. It is not on us, but God.

We understand that just because our hearts have been transformed, we will still make mistakes. It is impossible to be perfect on our own, as we have a fallen human nature. We must try our best, yet let God be the perfecter of our faith. Since we cannot do it on our own, Jesus shows us what to do to get help. Matthew 6:13 states, "And lead us not into temptation but deliver us from the evil one." Maybe you are addicted to a particular sin. Getting rid of this is not easy. It is only through God's help that we can avoid falling into temptations and traps. Every day we need to be saying thank you, asking for help and forgiveness. Notice where the focus is located. It is not on us, but God.

Did you notice I finished the last half of the Lord's Prayer first? The last half shows us different types of praying. I did that for a reason. I want us to look at the way Jesus prayed and understand where his desire was located. He did not ask about the things of this world but of the souls and the relationships.

When we first start in a relationship, we are typically selfish and try to get what we want. John 14:13–14 states, "And I will do whatever you ask in my name, so that the Father may be glorified in the Son. If you ask Me anything in My name, I will do it." It would be so easy to take this out of context and just start asking God for any of your wants. I want a million dollars, in your name. I would really like to have that special job, in your name. Help me win the contest, in your name.

Let us improve our communication and put the verses into context. This does not mean we can ask for anything we want. It means we can ask for anything he wants. As we grow in our relationship, our wants become his wants. What does he want? We notice in his prayer that he never lost his focus on the difference between Earth and heaven. He never cared about earthly treasure because he knew he was not going to stay. We lose our focus all of the time. He wanted his disciples to teach and lead others to Christianity. He was saying that if it helps you lead them, then ask for it and I will help.

As the relationship grows, lives transform. Our love for the other person in the relationship makes us want to please them more than ourselves.

When Jesus teaches them how to pray, he says, "Your kingdom come, your will be done, on Earth as it is in Heaven."[4] We should constantly search the will of God. This is the biggest purpose in prayer. Prayer is about aligning our will with God's will.

He is not a magic genie who is willing to grant wishes. I would not expect him to give me a million dollars just because I ask it in his name. I would not expect him to let me score a touchdown just because I ask it in his name. We are free to go to God with the desires of our hearts, but we must continue to work toward having a heart for God. Our will should be his will.

We must continually develop our prayer life to get better. We must keep trying to have our heart transformed toward good. Good communication helps the relationship grow and mature. Remember, a stronger relationship makes our lives better. To develop good communication, study the Lord's Prayer and work on your prayer life. Read how other saints in the Bible prayed. Actively listen, and make sure you are developing those good communication skills.

4. Matt 6:10.

CHAPTER 13

The Bumpy Road

(You Are Not Alone or Abandoned)

OUR DAUGHTER WAS SIXTEEN, and a junior in high school. We started looking at colleges for her to attend in the near future. We attended several campus tours, which we loved because they would give us free stuff. I cannot tell you how much university swag we scored that summer. She wanted to know more about Rice University, so we packed our bags and took a three-day trip from Oklahoma City to Houston. We had a great time. We took the college tour, saw some Houston sights, and took in a Rice football game.

On the way back, it was about noon when we were driving by Fort Worth, Texas, and we decided to stop for lunch. My daughter wanted Mexican food so I suggested Joe T. Garcias. She looked it up on her phone because she had never been there and it looked like a fantastic restaurant with delicious food. We agreed and turned off the interstate. I had her look up the address on her phone and then have the Global Positioning System (GPS) give us directions.

I do not know what we did before GPS. What a great invention. I used to have a paper road map to get me around but that did not provide information about a particular restaurant or shopping outlet. I can distinctly remember getting lost several times. My wife has a running joke of calling me "wrong-way Rick." When we go on vacation, we would use the GPS to get around but I am always in the wrong lane when it comes time to turn. I might be in the left lane and it wants me to turn right, or vice versa. Then I have to find a spot to turn around and get back on course.

I do not always like to follow GPS directions word for word to get me to my desired destination. Sometimes I like to take back roads because they have fewer cars and are less stressful. The problem with taking back roads is you never know the condition of the road. They are not always in the best condition like the main roads. They might have potholes making them bumpier and, therefore, they tear up your vehicle. Sometimes we run into dead-end streets where we can run into trouble.

For the life of me, to this day, I do not know what went wrong. I took an exit off Interstate 35W and things went from good to bad in rapid time. I must have missed the turn or gone the wrong way without realizing. We ended up in a part of North Fort Worth that was not a good part of town. I would not be able to find that place again if I tried.

In North Fort Worth, Texas, we faced a situation in which we were uncomfortable. We went down a dead-end street and were lost. I was worried. I told my daughter to get on the GPS and get us out of there the fastest way possible. The roads we went down were all in terrible condition and I longed for the restaurant. Obviously, we made it out to tell our story and Joe T. Garcias was delicious, but I will never forget that experience.

That is similar to the road we travel with Jesus. I look at the Bible in two ways. First, the Bible is the very thing that shows us who God is. We learn that the book, from start to finish, is about the life of Jesus. We learn about salvation and love. We learn about God's characteristics. We learn what our savior had to go through to have a relationship with us. It is a great piece of literature and I am thankful to those who took the time to write it and to those who took the time to copy it.

Second, the Bible gives us advice of how to live our life so we reach our destination safely. In a way, it is our GPS. I will call it a *God Positioning System*. It tells us to take this road and turn that way. It tells me when I have arrived at the place it wants me to currently be. All we have to do is follow its directions and we will reach our destination safely.

What is our destination? The GPS is guiding us to the ultimate restaurant. A place which has been prepared for us.[1] Heaven's buffet where the fatted calf has been prepared and the bounty is plentiful.[2] It is guiding us to a place where everything is sweeter. It is guiding us home.

The problem with this system is that we have free will. This means we can choose to follow the GPS or not. Instead of letting Jesus take the wheel,

1. John 14:3.
2. Luke 15:23.

I insist on doing the driving. The smoothest way is the straight and narrow path, but sometimes we choose a path we think we would like better. A path that is less hectic. A path that we think will be less stressful.

With our spiritual GPS, we cause problems for ourselves by taking turns that go against what it is telling us. We choose a path the GPS did not give us. We choose to go against its direction. When we go in a direction opposite of God, we are sinning. God is telling me to go down a particular path and I say no. I choose to go the way I want. It is not that we do not have choices in life. We can have choices yet still follow God's path.

What is God's path? I have heard many people say they were searching for the will of God for their life. I heard this mostly when I was younger and even said it myself. People are looking for some kind of sign, as if God will give us some miracle to tell us he wants us to work at a particular job. That is until we get a sign that we should work at a job we really would not want, and then we look for another sign. We do not have to see a sign to know the will of God. The Bible tells us what the will of God is. We can work in any career and do the will of God. The will of God is praying, doing good, loving, etc.

We all struggle with sin. Maybe you have something in your life in which you have a hard time. You might not want it in your life, but you cannot seem to get rid of it. You choose to follow that path instead of the way God would have you travel. As a result, we end up down roads that are worse for us. We put ourselves in peril, sometimes wondering if we are going to survive. The roads are bumpier.

I have a problem with people that say you are not going to heaven because you committed some sin. We are all sinners. That is the very reason Christ died for us. If we were not sinners then Christ on the cross would have been senseless. We go to heaven if we have a relationship with Jesus. Only he can see a person's heart. After we develop a relationship with Jesus, one accidental sin does not mean we are condemned forever. Should we ask forgiveness? Absolutely, yes! We cannot continue in our sin as if nothing is wrong. That displays a selfish heart. It is not a heart after God's heart. Yet, we need to get away from the idea that I sinned and am doomed forever. In my marriage, I have messed up plenty of times. My wife and I are still married. My daughter has messed up several times, but she is still a part of the family. Heck, I have messed up with my daughter several times, yet she has not disowned me. We do not lose a relationship because we mess up. Jesus does not abandon us because we mess up.

Sometimes we treat God as if he is there for us and there is no reciprocation. We just go driving aimlessly from here to there, not caring about his direction. When we do this, we sometimes keep a selfish attitude, yet say we are in a relationship with Jesus by stating we are Christians. I have the GPS on so he is with me, but I am not listening to his direction. We could lie and say we want to stay in a relationship even though we only care about ourselves. If the relationship is true, we should want to stop sinning and instead think less of ourselves and more of God. God, what do you want? God, how can I please you? In what direction do you want me to travel?

If my wife did not want me to watch pornography, yet I said I was going to anyway, I would expect her to get mad at a minimum and, at most, leave the relationship. Not because she no longer wants to be in the relationship, but because what kind of relationship is it when one of the persons is just selfish? What I would really be stating is that I do not care about the relationship as much as my wants. Does that kind of a relationship make sense? Yet that is how we sometimes treat God.

Proverbs 4:14 states, "Do not set foot on the path of the wicked or walk in the way of evildoers." Being human, we have a fallen nature. We are selfish and want things our way, so we do things differently than God would have us do.

We may have gone down a wrong road, but do not forget that we are still driving the car. We are still traveling down the road. God still wants us to make it to the restaurant. What does he do? He continues to give us directions. Maybe this time we will follow his instructions. We are still attempting to get to the restaurant. The key is that we never lose our faith in God's ability to direct us.

Those bumpy roads may cause us a flat tire, making us wonder if we will make the restaurant. I might consider this a person who gets involved with things they should not have and is overtaken by them. An example would be pornography. Pornography is greatly addictive and changes a person's mind over time. It might not start bad, but it has a way of destroying lives.

Maybe we are still driving but those dead-end roads may pull us away from continuing to drive to the restaurant. What would happen if we fall in love with a person who does not believe in God? This would be like a back seat driver, telling us their directions are better than God's directions. There is a chance that other person will turn to God but there is the chance you will be pulled away from God and stop driving to the buffet.

Your driving habits might be risky. Be careful. We only have so much time before we run out of gas. If we run out of gas, we cannot make the restaurant. This would be a situation where we continue to live our way instead of God's way until the end of our lives. Then it is too late.

When somebody or something pulls us away from God, it can be hard to get back on track. Getting a flat from those potholes is like letting sin prevent us from traveling down God's road. When this happens, it does not mean Jesus has abandoned us. We might feel like he has. We might go our own way for a while, but God does not forego his pursuit. When I turn the wrong way, the GPS says, "Recalculating," and gives me a new road to get me back on track. God does the same thing for us. When we turn a way that is opposite of his guidance, God does not abandon us. We are not condemned for all eternity. We just need to look in the book (GPS) and get back to the better road. God recalculates our route to lead us back to the proper path.

Our path may look different than it did before, but that does not mean it is now worse. Sometimes we look back at our history and think of the roads we should have taken. Hindsight is 20/20. We regret taking the wrong road and wish we could be back on that original road. Understand, God has recalculated and now has you on a different path. That previous road may be worse for you now. We need to learn to enjoy the road the Lord has us on now. He will guide you safely.

I think back to Peter. Peter was a fisherman. In the book of Luke, chapter 22, it tells the story of Peter denying Jesus. He let other people pull him away. He felt so bad that he wept bitterly.[3] He hit a bump in the road, which caused him to have a flat tire for three days. Then Jesus shows up. He was able to get a new tire and get back on the road. Peter decided to follow Jesus' path. Jesus recalculated his route. Peter became a great preacher, leading thousands to Christ. Instead of catching fish, he now was catching men. His road looked different than it had three days before, but Peter embraced it. We need to fix the flat, as quickly as possible, and get back on the road. We need to quit going our way, repent, and follow his paths.

Ideally, we should always follow God's guidance. Following does not guarantee there will be no bumps in life. You might be persecuted for following its guidance. We need to grow our attitudes to a different understanding. Even if our lives feel worse for following God, we are still so much better off for doing so. Living a life closer to God is so much

---

3. Luke 22:54–62.

better than having the luxuries of this world. We can have joy no matter our circumstances.

The problem is that we keep making wrong turns. As such, the roads we take are going to be a lot rougher than we want them to be. So many roads out there are not good for us. So many roads out there we should not take. Matthew 7:13 states, "Enter through the narrow gate. For wide is the gate and broad is the way that leads to destruction, and many enter through it." God wants us to be on the proper roads but he lets us decide to follow or not. It is truly amazing when you think about how many times we choose our way instead of God's way and he does not abandon us. He shows us how to recalculate to our destination. His grace is incredible.

Everybody takes the bumpy roads in their lives. For some reason, we just cannot avoid doing the wrong things. Do not fear. There is good news. The bumpy roads give us the motivation to continually recalculate and search out God. The bumpy roads scare us into wanting to change. The bumpy roads help us understand how much help we need. The bumpy roads show us that we cannot find it on our own. The bumpy roads show us his grace. We may not like them, but we need to thank God for the bumpy roads.

CHAPTER 14

Game Night

(The Importance of Following a Standard)

WHEN YOU GO OUT to the store and purchase a board game, you bring it home excited to get started playing. Maybe you saw it advertised on television and thought it looked fun. Maybe you played it with a friend who owned the game and decided to get the game for yourself. After unwrapping the game, you want to start playing the game right away but have a decision to make. Do I read the rules and make sure I am doing this right? Do I play it the way I currently think it should work?

It can be very hard to sit down and read the rules when you are excited to get started. I know people who never read the rules, whether that be for a board game, a sport, fixing things around the house, or assembling Christmas presents. When I played tennis, I once played against a person who crossed the baseline on every serve. As he was tossing the ball in the air, he would step forward. That is an illegal move. He did not have any problem with it. The closer you get to the net, the greater advantage you have. The rule is in place to keep things fair. Stop it!

I can understand. Reading the rules is boring. Maybe you saw them playing it on television and think you understand. How much different could it be from that? My friend plays the game and they taught me how to play. Surely they read the rules. Besides, is it not just logical?

I call these people troublemakers. Usually an argument ensues about right and wrong. They are usually type "A" personalities and arguing with them can be impossible. They typically think they know it all and it usually creates problems for others when they are not playing correctly.

I do not remember who taught me how to play the game but we liked to play *Monopoly* when I was young. I distinctly remember playing for long periods. After a while, and not being any closer to a winner, I would start thinking of how I could throw the game because I was tired of playing. Sometimes we would push it off to the side, making sure to not upset the board, and come back to it later. Patience is a virtue, but that is ridiculous.

One day, while we were playing, I decided to read the rules. We were playing many parts of the game incorrectly. For example—we played that if you were in jail, you could not collect rent if somebody landed on your property. Not true according to the rules. I am not sure what led us to do this but we had been playing incorrectly for years.

When you play correctly, Hasbro says a typical game should last between sixty and ninety minutes. That is a good game night. Not days. I do not have statistics to back this up but I see *Monopoly* played incorrectly more than any other game.

Monopoly is not the only game played incorrectly. When we used to play billiards, we played a game called eight ball. After making all of the stripes or solids, as appointed, we were taught you had to call where the eight ball would be pocketed. If it went in any other pocket than the one you called, then you lost the game. This is not a true rule. These are not the only games played incorrectly. I would think people have been playing games like *Clue*, *Uno*, and chess incorrectly for years. Where does this stuff come from?

In the game *Monopoly*, the creator wrote out a set of rules to follow. They knew the game better than the people who would be playing the game. They understood why certain rules had to be written the way they were. Even if they did not make sense to you, it was the best way to play the game. If you truly want to know the game and play it correctly, and you wish to be successful and win, you need to read the rules.

We have a set of rules in life also. Life is not only a board game, but there is a second game of life called reality. The air our lungs breathe, the blood the heart pumps, and the brain that controls movement are the tools used to play this game. Just like *Monopoly*, we have been given instruction on how to play this game. These rules are handed down to us from God. People who communicated with God wrote this stuff down. We call this standard handbook the Bible. These rules teach us how to play so that we can succeed. These rules help us get to the finish line. These rules help us win the game of life. How do they do this?

The Bible helps us understand who Jesus is. A relationship with Jesus is the only way to win the game. John 14:6 states, "I am the way and the truth and the life. No one comes to the Father except through me." The entire instruction book, from start to finish, is about him. The Old Testament is full of stories concerning the relationship between God and people, but it is not just a bunch of great stories.

There are hundreds of prophecies showing us who the Messiah would be. The first prophecy of Jesus comes in the third chapter of Genesis. In the New Testament, Jesus' lineage is traced. The New Testament is full of stories concerning the relationship between God and people, but it is not just a bunch of great stories. It shows us how Jesus fulfilled the law and is truly the Messiah we needed. It also shows us the beginning of the church, showing us God. Through the Bible, we learn the proper way to play our reality game, just like *Monopoly*, whose rules are given to us by the creator. If we wish to know the proper way to play, and we wish to know the Savior and win this game, we need to read the rules.

Just like *Monopoly*, many of us do not follow these rules. Why do we ignore the rules? There could be many reasons. Maybe we were never given a set of rules to follow. It is possible to get the board game and have the rules accidentally left out of that particular set. Could you imagine if the game creators just put the game in a box without inserting rules to follow? People would just make up whatever rules they wanted. The game would be chaotic and there would be a lot of cheating accusations. That actually sounds a lot like our society.

Living our life is similar. If we did not follow any set of rules, or a particular standard, we would certainly fall into chaos, with every individual just behaving the way they wanted, even to the point of being unfair to others around them. Actually, there would be no such thing as fair and unfair because you could only have a sense of fair if you had a standard to follow. That would not stop people from calling others unfair. You cannot cheat if you do not have a rule to follow. People do not want you to shove your morality on them. What standard of morality are they following? They are making up their own. That is because they are not following the standard God has given us to follow.

This would be the equivalent of a person who has never been told the story of Jesus and has never had the chance to read the Bible. This is sad to me. Could you imagine being given the game *Monopoly* with no instruction book, and nobody told you how to play the game? The game would not make sense. You would quickly make up your own rules because we cannot live in a world that does not make sense.

The person who never had a Bible to read would do the same thing in the game of life. Life would not make sense. They would play the game, wondering what the purpose of life really is, making up their own rules in an attempt to make sense of it. When everybody just creates their own rules, then nobody is playing by the same rules. As a result, society breaks down instead of flourishing. God gave us these standards

Maybe we are too lazy and just want to play the game. This is typical in many games. This is similar to the person who never received the rules. They would make up their own rules leading to dysfunction. This person has access to the Bible but chooses not to read it. There is no way to find that all-important Jesus relationship, which will get us to the finish line, without reading about him. Everything a person needs to know to win the game is available to them, yet they choose to not read the instructions. How sad.

Maybe we think others know how to play the game, so we have them teach us. This happens quite a bit. Many games we learn because we were with friends who wanted to enjoy the game with us. They told us how to play and we trusted them. That is how I initially learned to play *Monopoly*. Guess what? They taught me the incorrect way and I believed them. I think we can see how this can be a problem as many of us still play the game incorrectly.

The same thing happens with God. Maybe your parents or a good friend taught you. Maybe you sat under a preacher who taught you. These are people you trust, even with your life. Did they teach you correctly? How would you ever know without reading the instructions? Your friend might have good intentions, yet still teach you incorrectly. I played *Monopoly* incorrectly until I read the rules. Some are willing to sit in a pew on Sunday morning and listen to the pastor speak without ever digging into the material for themselves. There have been many who have been led astray this way. We need to take time to learn for ourselves. Trust the friend but double check for your sake.

I talked with a bank teller one day about counterfeit money. I asked how they trained her to locate fake money. She said they did not do that. That took me by surprise, so I asked why. She said they are taught what real money looks like. If something comes across the desk that does not look the way they are taught then it should be examined further. Understanding the truth helps us recognize the false. If we read the rules, and learn the truth, then we will be able to discern the truth or falsehood of others. Listening to others tell us false things instead of learning the truth for ourselves leads us to play incorrectly.

Maybe we think the rules are stupid and the game would be much more fun if we played by our own rules. I get that. More so, when you are young, you may want to disobey the rules because it is fun or exciting. This is, more or less, what sin is. Sin is doing things our way instead of Jesus' way. We know the proper thing to do but choose our way instead. If we truly wish to have a relationship with Jesus, then we must choose to follow the rules provided by the Creator. Matthew 16:26 states, "What good will it be for someone to gain the whole world, yet forfeit their soul?" We may fool ourselves and think we are winning the game, playing by our rules. What we are really doing is losing, but the finish will be a surprise.

Some people play by other rules that are different from those the creator intended because the creator's rules do not make sense to them and they think they know better. I can see how somebody may think this way. There is a lot of stuff in the Bible that is difficult to understand. As a result, people willfully disobey. When I talk to these people, it is usually because of a feeling. They say things like, "I do not feel that can be correct." Just because we do not understand does not mean it is wrong. We need to follow the rules, or the standard, set before us.

How can we make sense of it? How about calling out for help. We do not have to understand everything to understand our depravity and need for Jesus. We do not have to understand everything about Jesus to have a relationship with him. Imagine if you could call the creators of the game *Monopoly*. You could ask them about those rules that do not make sense and have them explain why those rules are important. The same thing happens with the Bible but we must first establish that all-important relationship with Jesus. We must have contact with him. First Corinthians 2:14 states, "The person without the Spirit does not accept the things that come from the Spirit of God but considers them foolishness, and cannot understand them because they are discerned only through the Spirit." When we accept Jesus as our Savior, the Holy Spirit helps us in our understanding. We need first accept the gospel, and then read the rules and study its words.

In reality, we do not know better than the Creator does. We fool ourselves because we cannot fully understand the Creator's ways. The problem is that we need to come to Jesus as he is and not water down the gospel to fit our understanding.

There may be many reasons we ignore the rules, but the rules are there for a reason. A particular rule may not make sense but, when put together with the rest, helps us see the big picture. Making up rules leads us down a path of losing. The rules are there to help us play the game in a fair way. The rules teach us how to win the game. We act foolish when we do not read and follow the rules. There is nothing more important than finding Jesus, and following the rules is the way to do this.

SECTION 3

The Married Life

CHAPTER 15

The Marriage Ceremony

(A Covenant between Two)

BEV AND I WERE married on September 23, 1995. It was one of the happiest days of my life. I remember Bev walking down the aisle toward me. All I could think about was how beautiful she looked. From a distance we heard, "She looks like an angel." It was my cousin's five-year-old son, Tyler. He was the ring bearer. I was in such a good mood that everything that happened that day was great.

For all of the things that went right that day, we had plenty go wrong. Back by the dressing room, my wife heard them say Tyler had lost the rings. I heard about this days later and never did find out if that was a true event or somebody trying to tease by saying it loud enough for Bev to hear. Our pastor messed up the process. The ceremony did not look like the rehearsal. I do not think he ever realized he messed up and we never told him. To top it off, my groomsmen were able to pull off a great prank, embarrassing me. With all of those issues, here is what I remember. It was one of the best days of my life. I was very happy. It did not matter that things were not perfect. I could not believe this great person was going to marry me. I was so happy; the bad things did not even stress me. I was so overjoyed. It was the day I joined my best friend in marriage.

On that day in September, we stood before witnesses and declared our giving to one another. We made a covenant with one another. I promised certain things and she promised certain things. A covenant is a relationship where two people make promises to one another to reach a common goal.

This is a covenant unlike any other. From that moment on, we were one team that nobody was going to come between.

After we have studied Jesus for a sufficient amount of time, we find out if we want to spend the rest of our lives with him. If so, we ask him to come into our lives and transform us. From that moment on, we are no longer Jew or gentile. We are different. We are Christians. We are committed for the rest of our lives. We should be growing in the relationship.

How does this work? It is hard to believe, but it is simple. There are only two things we need to focus on to be reconciled to God. Romans 10:9–10 states, "If you confess with your mouth that Jesus is Lord and believe in your heart that God raised him from the dead, you will be saved. For with the heart one believes and is justified, and with the mouth one confesses and is saved." That is it! When you get married to your spouse, you stand before witnesses and say, "I do." You are confessing with your mouth that you agree to this covenant between you and your spouse. When you confess, "Jesus is Lord" to others, you agree to a covenant between you and Jesus. It is not about accomplishing a bunch of good works. It is about putting your trust in him. Just as Bev put her trust in me, I put my trust in her, and we put our trust in Jesus.

I know I just said it was simple, but that is just the marriage ceremony. At the ceremony, we speak with our mouths and agree to join. In a way, that is lip service. It can be easy to say words. Do you really mean the promises you made? Now the hard part comes. Now we have to dedicate our lives to the other person.

As we grow in this new relationship, we become more and more unselfish. It is truly an amazing thing to witness. I have now been married for over twenty-five years and I can honestly say I want so much more for my wife and child than I ever do for myself. I have learned that it brings me joy to make them happy. The same thing happened with Jesus. As the relationship has grown, I want more of what he wants, forsaking myself.

When I married Bev, I entered into a covenant with her. I made promises to her and she made promises to me. I promised to be true to her in good times and bad. We promised to stick by each other for better or for worse. Well, we have seen the good times and the bad times. We have seen the better times and we have seen the worse times. My wife is there to rejoice with me when things are going well and cry with me when things are going bad. So far, over twenty-five years going strong. I hope we will stay together for another twenty-five years.

We should say the same thing about our relationship with Jesus. It does not matter if we are going through good times or bad times. Sometimes when we go through bad times, we might blame God and get angry with him. Would you do that with your spouse? Our problems are not his fault. We should want to bring God closer so that we can be comforted. We agree to stay true to him forever. It does not matter what we are going through.

I went on to say I would love her and honor her all of my life. Love is a choice. I am choosing to get up every day and love my wife. When we agree to a covenant with Jesus, we should do the same. We will love him and honor him for the rest of our lives.

Now we understand that as a part of loving him, we want to please him. Jesus spoke to his disciples about this. John 14:15 states, "If you love me, keep my commands." In other words, he would like it if we would accomplish the things he wants us to do. When we hear the word "command," it brings to mind imagery of a tyrant or dictator forcing us to do their will, but do not forget the first part of that sentence: "If you love me." The things we have already learned about him while we were dating include: He wants us to be obedient and sacrifice our lives for him. He wants us to teach others his way and baptize them. He wants us to gather with other Christians and lift each other up in faith. He wants us to communicate with him. He wants us to follow his paths. If we love him, we will gladly do these things. We will gladly make a choice to love him. If we do not love him, then why would we want to be in a relationship with him?

Matthew 4:17 states, "Repent, for the kingdom of heaven has come near." "Repent" means to feel regret or remorse about sin. It means to turn and go the opposite direction. Without God in our lives, we are traveling down a road where we live for ourselves. That may not be unethical or immoral behavior but it does not mean we are following God's paths. When we repent, we turn and go in the opposite direction, live for God, and forsake ourselves. As we stand before him, this is our promise to him.

Let us not forget that a relationship is a two-way street. We have talked about the promises we have made to God. What about the promises God makes to us? We are not going into this relationship one-sided.

I cannot tell you how many times I have seen people depressed about God because of something bad going on in their lives. Some are poor and think life has been unfair to them, and they cannot understand why God would do this to them. Some suffer great loss and cannot understand. Any time we think God is not being fair, we need to take a step back and look at what he promises us. Hint: it is not money, worldly success, or even earthly protection.

He promises to give us strength. Isaiah 40:29 states, "He gives strength to the weary and increases the power of the weak." He did not say we would not have to face the world. He did not say we would not have to face temptation. He did not say we would not go through tough times or not face persecution. I think sometimes we have this thought that if we trust in Jesus he will take care of us in a way that is not troublesome. I do not read that anywhere. We will still have problems but he does not want us to face the world alone. If we go forward with just our own strength, we will fail. Satan is too powerful for us on our own. We need to place our hearts and hopes on things greater than this world. If we put him first, he will carry us through the difficult times. Isaiah 41:10 states, "So do not fear, for I am with you; do not be dismayed, for I am your God. I will strengthen you and help you; I will uphold you with my righteous right hand." This is a promise he has made. This is an agreement as part of our covenant.

He promises to give us wisdom. He did not promise that statements, which were not wise from the world, would not bombard us. James 1:5 states, "If any of you lacks wisdom, you should ask God, who gives generously to all without finding fault, and it will be given to you." James has been telling the church that we ought to aim for perfection. He also understood that, being human, we still lack. He is encouraging his people to reach out and ask God for help. He is not just talking about being intelligent. This is not about becoming a great theologian or getting God's help to get through school. You have to study to receive that. He is speaking about the Lord. He is speaking about how it is wise for us to look upon him in the proper way. We are asking for divine wisdom. He promises to give it as a part of this covenant.

He promises to meet our needs in this covenant. He did not promise that we would not struggle. Philippians 4:19 states, "And my God will meet all your needs according to the riches of his glory in Christ Jesus." What are your needs? Do you know what they are? We, personally, might think we know. If I am hungry, I have a need for food. If I am thirsty, I have a need for water. Does that mean that if I am too stupid to take food and water into the desert and I become hungry and thirsty, God will magically make food and water appear? Maybe not. If I am a big enough idiot to go into the desert without food and water, then I am not going to expect God to take care of my needs. There is a chance that I will die. If I have a bad heart, will

God provide a new heart? Maybe not. Have you noticed? We all die. Maybe we do not understand what we truly need. Maybe food, water, and shelter are not what we need. It is true that those are earthly needs, but I do not see him saying that here. He does not promise to keep us alive forever. Notice, it is according to the riches of his glory in Jesus Christ. The only thing I absolutely need is a relationship with Jesus. If I have that, he will take care of me. My true needs are going to be met. There is nothing this life has to offer that is any more important than a covenant with Jesus.

He promises to purify us. First John 1:9 states, "If we confess our sins, he is faithful and just and will forgive us our sins and purify us from all unrighteousness." This is still something that amazes me. I believe it to be true, but it still amazes me. I do not know how this works but this is how I view it. Sinning is like putting a rip in your clothes. After a while, your clothes are so tattered you look like a bum and are unfit to sit with royalty. Isaiah 61:10 states, "For he has clothed me with the garments of salvation, he has covered me with the robe of righteousness." Revelation 7:9 states, "Standing before the throne and before the Lamb, clothed in white robes." Zechariah 3:4 states, "And the angel said to those who were standing before him, 'Remove the filthy garments from him.' And to him he said, 'Behold, I have taken your iniquity away from you, and I will clothe you with pure vestments.'" Revelation 3:5 states, "The one who is victorious will, like them, be dressed in white. I will never blot out the name of that person from the book of life, but will acknowledge that name before my Father and his angels." All of these verses make me think that we will be given robes of righteousness. Those old, dirty, torn rags of ours will be thrown out. If we put our trust in Jesus, he promises to make us clean. Only he can provide that type of robe—the type of robe that gives eternal life. Only Jesus can supply us with this robe.

Eternal life. Can you imagine? God wants to have a loving relationship for eternal life. We should want that same thing. It has been a blessing to have my family in my life. We have laughed, shared, given, lost, and loved. Although it has been great, there is no greater blessing than having a covenant with Jesus. My life has been so much richer because of it. Jesus promised me eternal life with the one I love. My prayer is that you also find Jesus and learn the love he has to offer. Your life can change forever.

CHAPTER 16

Adoption

(The Process of Becoming a Child of God)

WE ALL GO THROUGH good and bad times. It is just a part of living. My wife and I have had many good times to celebrate. However, our family has had a couple of times in our history that stand out as particularly hurtful. It is incredible how these times affect your lives. I have seen grief at its highest level and disappointment to a great degree. It is also the time you learn what each other are made of, leaning on each other, and growing stronger in love.

My wife and I were married in 1995. For the first few years, we were just getting to know each other and attempting to enjoy married life. We took several trips around the country. It was more about just being together and falling in love. After a few years, we decided we wanted to have a child.

If there was anybody perfect to have kids, it was my wife. That is the biggest thing she wanted in life. In high school, she took courses at our vocational center pertaining to taking care of kids. She ran her own day care. She has watched other people's kids ever since we have been together. She has worked in the public schools and taught the little ones in our church. This is her gift. This is her burden.

What is one of the worst things that can happen to a person who desires to have kids? We had been trying to conceive without luck. In the summer of 1998, we decided to be checked by doctors. It turned out that we have medical issues making the chances of pregnancy incredibly low. So low the doctors thought it impossible. The news was enough to send us into a minor depressive state.

The very same week we got that news I found out my mother had been admitted to the hospital and was going to have surgery. Talk about a double whammy. We drove two hours to be with her after she got out of surgery. Her lungs had been damaged due to a ruptured esophagus. She lay in intensive care for a week before succumbing to her problems and passing away.

My mother was somebody I was close enough with that I would have talked to her about our inability to have kids, but she was gone. My wife and I were the only ones that knew for a period.

During this time, our best friends were pregnant with their second baby. Although we were hurting inside, I still was not jealous. I was still happy for them. My loss did not mean I wanted them to suffer. It was a little awkward as it felt like they wanted to celebrate but could not do so in front of us. I do not remember them telling us this, but it just had a feeling about it. I felt like I was taking some of their joy away because they did not want to rub it in, knowing we could not conceive. I wanted them to experience as much joy as they could and they did not want their birth to bring us down. It was a difficult time. Let us just say, the summer of 1998 was not that great for Bev and I. There was much to be desired.

For a brief time, we did explore our options. We knew we wanted kids but we did not want to rush into making a bad decision. In the fall of 1999, we took a trip to Hawaii. It was during this trip that our future came into focus. We discussed the issues and determined our next roles. Instead of spending thousands in fertility treatments to have our own child, we felt it was more important for us to try to help kids that already existed, but needed somewhere to turn. We considered adopting. We looked into that process and came close to going that route. We went back home and signed up to become foster parents.

The process to certify as a foster parent was interesting. We had to take classes, get our home inspected, have a huge background check, and make sure our home was a safe place. It is funny. If we had had our own biological kids, we would not have had to make our home as safe as the state required of us at this time.

We were certified as foster parents in May of 2000. It still took a couple of months, but the first child came to us in September. Emily was four months old. Her birth parents were going through some rough times and no other family members could take care of her. My wife fell in love on day one and all I could think was how devastating it was going to be for her when this child would have to go back to their home. Had we gotten in over our heads? I did not think we were going to fall in love. Were we setting ourselves up for continual grief? Was this a mistake?

Being a foster parent is not easy. The parents sometimes hate you because they look at you as the one who is keeping their child away from them. When the child returns home, even though we know it is going to happen, it hurts.

We fostered a few kids over the next few years. We were certified for only two children at any given time, so it was not as if we had a ton of kids come through our house. Typically, our foster children stayed one to six months before they went back home. Bev and I hurt every time a child left. I can only imagine what their biological parent was going through.

Most foster kids come from bad situations. Either the child or the parent has problems. Sometimes they feel they cannot live together anymore. Sometimes they want to live together but they are apart for safety or legal reasons. Sometimes it is through an incredibly hard loss. Usually it was hard on the families. Nobody wants to lose his or her family. It was hard on us when they would go back to their parents. Although hard to say good-bye, we took comfort in knowing we were making a difference in the lives of these people. At least I hoped we were making a difference in their lives. Believing we were making a difference is the only way we were able to keep it going. Again, a tough job, sometimes thankless, but necessary.

The only child we had in our care that did not go back was Emily. She was the first to enter our house. Two years after entering our lives it was determined that she would go through the adoption process. Typically, the state would look for other family members in an attempt to keep the child in the family. With Emily, it just so happened that there was nobody in her family that could adopt her. By this time, we had fallen in love with her. There was no way we could let her go to another family. We stepped up and made her our child.

Adoption day. What an incredible day. We had family, friends, and state case workers in that court room. There must have been thirty or more people in that tiny space. The judge said he had just one requirement to finalize the adoption. I had to take everybody in that room out for ice cream. Obviously, he was kidding but I told him yes and was happy to do that. Then he announced, from that day forward, Emily would forever have our last name.

When you read a book, or watch a movie, or whatever, sometimes the words make a person cry. When you write a book, you read the same chapters over many times. Every time I think and read this story, I still cry.

My daughter thinks I cry too much, but my feelings in this situation are overpowering. I cannot tell you what it meant to me the day we adopted her.

Just like that, our hurt was gone. The tears were no longer tears of hurt, but tears of joy. Everybody came back to our house and we celebrated. We did not care that Emily was not our biological child. We had so much love for her and we dedicated our lives to her forever. We never even thought of her as anything else but ours. We told her about her adoption when we thought she was old enough to understand, but she says she does not think of us in any other way except as hers. She has no problem talking to other people about adoption, and it has actually brought up some interesting situations.

In the eyes of the law, adoption means she, on day one, became an heir to our estate. If we had other biological kids, she would have been an equal joint-heir to our estate. She is not just somebody we took care of. She is not just somebody who lives in our house and eats our food. She is a full-blown child of ours. She received a brand new birth certificate with our names listed as her parents. The law does not see her as not our biological child and we do not see her as anything less. Adoption is an incredible process.

Adoption is not something new. Its roots run deep. Romans 8:14–17 states, "For all who are led by the Spirit of God are sons of God. For you did not receive the spirit of slavery to fall back into fear, but you have received the Spirit of adoption as sons, by whom we cry, 'Abba! Father!' The Spirit himself bears witness with our spirit that we are children of God, and if children, then heirs—heirs of God and fellow heirs with Christ, provided we suffer with him in order that we may also be glorified with him."

Imagine that! We are joint heirs with Christ. God is our father. Heaven is our new home. We are never alone. He promises to love us forever. How great can it get? Luke 15:10 states, "In the same way, I tell you, there is rejoicing in the presence of the angels of God over one sinner who repents." Just like we celebrated the day Emily joined our family, heaven celebrates when just one person is saved.

Galatians 4:4–8 states, "But when the fullness of time had come, God sent forth his Son, born of woman, born under the law, to redeem those who were under the law, so that we might receive adoption as sons. And because you are sons, God has sent the Spirit of his Son into our hearts, crying, 'Abba! Father!' So you are no longer a slave, but a son, and if a son, then an heir through God. Formerly, when you did not know God, you were enslaved to those that by nature are not gods."

Notice how Paul says God redeemed us. To redeem means to obtain by paying a price. When we adopted Emily, we had fees to pay, such as court, attorney, clerk, etc. What are the fees for God to adopt us as his children? Galatians 3:13 states, "Christ redeemed us from the curse of the law by becoming a curse for us—for it is written, 'Cursed is everyone who is hanged on a tree.'" The cost of adoption was his very Son's life on the cross. He paid the greatest price anybody could pay. That should tell you how much he loves us.

John 1:12–13 states, "But to all who did receive him, who believed in his name, he gave the right to become children of God, who were born, not of blood nor of the will of the flesh nor of the will of man, but of God."

Adoption is rooted much more deeply in God's purpose than it is for humans adopting other humans. He knew from the beginning of time that this would be the plan. God wants to have a father/child relationship with us. The comparison is incredible.

This becomes even more amazing when we see how far apart we were. Just like the way most foster children come through some sort of bad situation, typically requiring special attention, we also come from bad situations, requiring a lot of attention. When my wife saw Emily for the first time, she saw this gorgeous little girl. It is not as if God found this cute, irresistible child and could not help himself. He saw us as sinful, evil beings, who would not be easy to deal with or take care of. Yet, he wanted to adopt us anyway, so he found a way to do that.

Can you imagine? What would you do if there were a teenager living on the street? They are homeless, dirty, destitute, and hopeless. They have a drug problem and an anger problem, and they steal from stores and fight to survive. Then one day somebody asks you to take him or her in and help him or her. That does not sound like a good time, yet that is how God saw us and wanted to take us in anyways.

We loved Emily before she was our child. God loves everybody even though we might not yet be his adopted children. Emily did not have to give us anything to be taken in. We loved her, wanted her, and gave her a home with no cost to her. When we accept what Jesus did for us on the cross, God calls us his children. We do not have to perform works to accomplish this. As God's children, we are joint heirs with Christ, and all that heaven has to offer is accessible to us. Our blood is now royal because our father is the king. We do not just live there. We do not just eat the food there. He loves us unconditionally. We are a part of the family of God. We are not a waste. We are royal. Let us never forget what that means.

CHAPTER 17

Changing Names

(The Gloriousness of Heaven)

WHEN YOU ARE GOING to have a child, one of the things you might do is to get a book of baby names and determine what you would like to name the child. Some people keep it simple and popular. Some go out on a limb and try to be trendsetters.

I do not know if you have ever given any thought to your name. You probably did not have any choice in the matter when your name was assigned. It was given to you by your parents or by some sort of caretaker. Maybe you liked the name, maybe you did not. I, personally, did not like my name. Looking through my genealogy, I should probably be happy. My family history included names like Alona, Basil, Delpha, Norvella, Clifton, Gaither, Willard, Otis, Claud, and Dora.

My official, given name is Ricky Krietemeyer. People do not believe me most of the time. They usually think it is something else like Richard and I use Ricky to shorten it. They usually ask me if I go by Rick or Ricky. It probably was not that bad as a kid but it does not seem like an adult's name. I think my mother, born in 1940 and raised in the fifties, liked Ricky Nelson and the name probably stuck with her. Side note: Ricky Nelson was born Eric Hillard Nelson. His parents called him Ricky on the *Ozzie and Harriet* show and he became famous as Ricky. I remember when Ricky Schroeder tried to drop the *y* from his name. He had grown up and was feeling the same way I did when I grew up. The way people reacted, you would have thought society was going to fall apart.

Then there is the last name Krietemeyer. My ancestors were of German descent, coming to America in the late nineteenth century. When they first arrived in the United States, the name had a second *i* in it. My ancestors spelled it "Krietemeier." Somebody thought it should look like an American name, so the *i* was changed to *y*. As if that did something big to it. The problem with this name is that nobody knows how to say it. Nobody can spell it. It is way too long. I am not sure how long it took me to learn how to spell it growing up but I have been spelling it for everybody else since. Even Siri on my phone cannot pronounce it properly. I tell people to take the remaining *i* out and try it. Then it makes more sense to them. I went into a profession, as a flight instructor, in which I had to sign my name all of the time. You try signing that long name several times a day. I started to understand why my doctor's signature was not legible when I received a prescription.

My uncle James gave everybody nicknames. From the time I was born, he called me Moose. That ended up being interesting because I was a runt when I was born premature. Later I became quite a big person. When I was young, O. J. Simpson had just finished a great football career and was running through airports for Hertz rental car. When O. J. was playing football, and broke free for a long run, they would yell, "The Juice is loose!" I can remember playing football in the backyard and my uncle yelling, "The Moose is loose!" I enjoyed that nickname. My parents never called me Moose. That was something only my uncle did on his own, so the nickname really did not stick.

After I became a pilot, I was flying a DC-9 for TWA and a situation came up in the back of the airplane. I was the first officer at the time. I did not even know what was happening but the captain came up to the cockpit and told me to follow him. We were still parked at the gate, preparing to leave. I got up and followed him, although I did not know what was happening. We went about half way back of the airplane and he stopped. What I found out a few moments later was that he had stopped just beyond a passenger that was hassling the flight attendants. He had been drinking before the flight and was now not cooperating. Where he stopped made me stand directly next to the person. I still did not know what we were doing. The captain said, "I want you off my plane now!" In other words, he put me in the position of the muscle. Now I understood what was going on and was wondering if I had just been thrown into a fight unknowing and unwilling. Fortunately, the man got up, gathered his belongings, and left the airplane without any more problems.

That was the beginning of the trip. The captain called me "the enforcer" for the rest of the trip. That is not the nickname I wanted.

When I became a safety inspector for the Federal Aviation Administration (FAA), I had the privilege of giving check rides to new flight instructors. I would meet them at the airport and give them an exam. This was a good and bad job. I loved that feeling when a person would pass and I had the privilege of giving them a brand new flight instructor certificate. A flight instructor certificate is something a pilot works very hard to get. It is not an easy program. Not only do you have to know how to fly, but you have to be able to teach others how to fly, and take responsibility for their safety. A flight instructor has to sign a pilot's logbook saying they can go solo. There are not many things that are more nerve-wracking than watching your student fly off and not being able to take over if they have a problem. The flight instructor certificate is a major milestone in their lives, worth celebrating. I also had to fail people sometimes, and that was hard.

One applicant wanted to learn more about me before their exam. They hoped to gain insight into how I give exams. He went into an online message board and asked if anybody knew anything about me, as he was about to take his check ride with me in a couple of weeks. Somebody, attempting to tease the nervous applicant wrote, "He's known as the 'Eliminator'. He has also been known to physically assault candidates in addition to pink-slipping them. There is good intel that he's killed at least five men in various bars and such around the globe while working as a 'contractor' for 'the company'. His pet peeve is people who under-dress for the checkride—wear a suit."[1] I thought that was funny. I printed the exchange and posted it in several places around work but the nickname, "The Eliminator," never took off.

I would think most people go through their lives without much thought of changing their name. We had a couple instances in our lives that made us think about name changes. We considered different names when we adopted our daughter. We were asked if we wanted it changed. We had the option to change it to whatever we wanted. Wow! Just imagine the damage you could do with that request. We chose to keep her name Emily. Emily is a name we liked. Emily is the name she was used to hearing. It just fit.

Another time we considered different names was when my wife and I were married. My wife had to decide what she would do with her last name. Traditionally, the bride would take the groom's last name. In today's society,

1. Written by WacoFan in "CFI Checkride."

there are many different options for the bride, including keeping her original name. To Bev, it did not seem like such a hard decision. I do think she wishes she could have married a person with a shorter last name, but she wanted to take my name in marriage and change it over to Krietemeyer.

The purpose of this book is to show correlations between our lives and the relationship we have with Jesus. In the Bible, we have correlation examples of what that relationship should look like. There are many verses referring to Jesus as the Bridegroom. The "church," or "children of god," is the bride. Does that mean that we are to receive a new name after salvation? Do we take Jesus' last name since he is the Groom? I do not even know what that name would be.

I never hated my name enough to go get it changed legally, but have you ever thought about the meaning of your name and if it fits? Names do not always fit their personality. As far as I am concerned, the name Ricky is only used for recordkeeping purposes. As I grew older, I began to wonder if that name truly fit me. I looked it up. The name Ricky is an English baby name. It is an abbreviation of Richard. There were several kings named Richard. The name means hard ruler, eternal ruler, and powerful. This was not me at all. For a lot of my life I was a weak, introverted follower.

I noticed there have been several people listed in the Bible who had their names changed. Abram became Abraham. Abraham means high father or father of many. This had been given to him by God to show his promise that Abraham would be the father of many nations. Sarai was changed to Sarah, which means mother of nations. Jacob was changed to Israel. Jacob meant heel grabber or supplanter. He cheated his brother out of his rights as the firstborn. Israel means one who has been strong against God. Jesus changed Simon's name to Peter, which means rock. Saul's name changed to Paul. He did this because Paul was Greek for the Jewish Saul. The Greek were the people with whom he was associating. There are others but they all had reasons for the name change. Although not comprehensive, a name change was usually done to establish a new identity that God wished them to embody.

The name Ricky means powerful ruler. I have no desire to be ruler over anything. There is only one person I wish to let rule in my life and that is Jesus. If I ruled, I would definitely make a mess of things. Because I have a boring life, I went on a search to find out who I am and what name may fit me best.

The first thing I thought about was how I fit with God. I knew God was king. I also knew I was a child of God's, being adopted and all. That must make me a prince. Maybe I should go around calling myself Prince Rick. After all, princes like William and Harry get a lot of attention. Could you imagine every Christian going around calling themselves prince or princess before their name? I was not so sure about that.

One day I came across the name Maven. Maven means one who is experienced or knowledgeable in a particular field. A Maven knows their subject inside and out and is often the person one would go to when you want to talk with an expert. Not only is a Maven a trusted expert but they seek to pass that knowledge on to others. This seemed to fit. First, I have been a pilot in many different settings including charter pilot, airline pilot, general aviation pilot, corporate pilot, etc. I have worked on and studied many different types of aircraft, regulations, and aviation-related topics. Not only have I tried to become an expert, I have taught as an instructor in many different aviation fields. I have been a flight instructor for over twenty-five years. I received a master's degree in aeronautical science. I have taught at the university level, in simulators, in actual aircraft, and on many different subtopics. I am passionate about helping others so that we have a safe aviation system. I do feel like I am a good instructor. Yes, Maven seemed to fit.

I can remember bringing this name up to my wife and sister-in-law one day. Behind the side snickering, they appeased me in my lunacy. My wife thought she would be snide and asked what my new last name would be. I thought for a moment and came up with the name Storm. This only took a couple of minutes, so not a lot of thought was given. There was no real significance behind the name Storm except that it was short, easy to say, and I thought it was a great last name for a pilot. I could just imagine saying "a storm is coming your way." I think I had just finished watching the *Fantastic Four* movie so it was probably just fresh in my mind as two of the main characters have that last name. That was it! My name would be Maven Storm. Again, side snickering at my lunacy. I never took it seriously enough to have it legally changed, but I have used it in certain situations like reserving a table at the local restaurant. The name is shorter, everybody can pronounce it, and the name fits with who I feel I truly am as a person.

When we join into this covenant with Jesus, the Holy Spirit provides us with gifts. These gifts can be found in the books of Isaiah, Romans, 1 Corinthians, Ephesians, and 1 Peter. I have studied those gifts, and I feel my gift from the Spirit to be that of teacher. Not because I have taught many aviation students. A teacher has the ability to take information and find a way to make that information affect another person's behavior and abilities. In aviation, that behavior change is to stop acting in an unsafe manner. The gift of teacher is given by the Spirit to help people see God in such a way that their behavior changes from an unsafe manner to that of a full follower. One of my philosophies is that if you want to learn, read. If you really want to learn, write. If you really, really want to learn, teach. I really, really want to learn about God.

I do not know if Maven is the name God would give me, but I do know I will receive a new name. Why? Because I am a new person. In Revelation 2:17 it states, "To the one who conquers I will give some of the hidden manna, and I will give him a white stone, with a new name written on the stone that no one knows except the one who receives it." Isaiah has several verses which talk about a name change that will last forever and is given by God. After this life is over, and we reach heaven, God will change our names. These names will be great because they are a gift from God. Just like the characters of the Bible, they will represent a changed identity, as we have made a change from sinful to holy. Receiving a new identity does not mean we give up our identity. The names he will give us will describe our identity. First Corinthians, chapter 15 gives us a good view of this new identity. Verses 48–49 state, "As was the man of dust, so also are those who are of the dust, and as is the man of heaven, so also are those who are of heaven. Just as we have borne the image of the man of dust, we shall also bear the image of the man of heaven."[2] We will take on the form of Christ.

I think of salvation as a changed identity. When I die, my name will be written in the Lamb's book of life. Daniel 12:1 states, "At that time Michael, the great prince who protects your people, will arise. There will be a time of distress such as has not happened from the beginning of nations until then. But at that time your people—everyone whose name is found written in the book—will be delivered."

Luke 10:20 states, "However, do not rejoice that the spirits submit to you, but rejoice that your names are written in heaven." Heaven is going to be glorious and knowing our name is written in his book forever is too incredible to put into words. Heaven is our home and it is going to be glorious.

---

2. 1 Cor 15:48–49.

CHAPTER 18

A New Home

(From Suffering to Perfection)

NEARLY TWO THOUSAND YEARS ago, the biggest event in human history took place. An event that changed the game. Jesus was a real person. He suffered and died for our sins. As he was hanging on the cross, there were two men dying next to him on their own crosses. Matthew 27:38 states, "Two rebels were crucified with him, one on his right and one on his left." Other versions call these men robbers.

In my opinion, crucifixion is about the worst type of death possible. The reason it was so horrific is because it usually lasted several days. It was usually slow and painful. The word "crucifixion" gives us our word "excruciating." It is gruesome. It does not just kill. It shames and sets an example to prevent others from committing similar crimes.

One of the criminals, hanging next to Jesus, hurled insults at him. He said, "Aren't you the Messiah? Save yourself and us!"[1] It reminds me of the way Satan tempted Jesus before his ministry began. Matthew 4:5–6 says, "Then the devil took him to the holy city and had him stand on the highest point of the temple. 'If you are the Son of God,' he said, 'throw yourself down.'" Jesus told him in verse 7, "Do not put the Lord your God to the test."[2] It appears Jesus now ignores the thief's comments. Why? This person was not repentant. Jesus is interested in people who will follow him, even through death.

1. Luke 23:39.
2. Matt 4:7.

The other criminal rebuked the first criminal. He understood he was guilty. He understood his punishment as just. He also understood that Jesus did not deserve punishment. Jesus did not commit a crime. The second man asked Jesus to remember him when Jesus went into his kingdom.[3] He understood he needed grace. He was repentant and, as such, wanted to have a relationship with Jesus.

Both of these men were guilty of crimes and sin and were suffering. God was right there. They had a final choice to make before they died. They could blame God for their suffering and ask for a wish, like the first person, or recognize they deserve punishment and cry out for mercy, like the second person. In the first, it is all about earthly help: I have troubles and I want out of them. Please God, come to my aid and make my earthly life better. The second is about eternal help: I know I have troubles, but do not forget me after this life is done.

This is a great picture of how we handle pain and suffering. We live in a fallen world. Satan has had such an effect, and evil exists everywhere. As a result, there will be suffering. Even if we do not commit a crime, we are just as guilty of sin. The majority will probably not die on a cross. Yet, we still go through hardships. We will lose jobs and struggle to make ends meet. We will get sick and encounter pain. We have people in our lives that die. We are insulted and offended. It hurts.

You also have God close and available. He is listening to you in your suffering. He is there to help. How will you speak to him? Will you get mad and curse God? Will you hurl insults at him unless he satisfies your worldly desires? Some see God as evil because he has power, yet does not give them what they want. Maybe you will be like the second person on the cross. Maybe you will see yourself as a sinful being and ask for mercy. What are you going to ask God for in your situation?

The first thief could not see past their earthly circumstances. This man is what some call the world. In other words, he did not really believe Jesus to be the king. He did not intend to follow Jesus. He did not care about anybody but himself. He would have served anybody if that person removed him from that cross.

We treat God this way sometimes. There are people who never do anything for Jesus until they are in trouble. Then they do not know where to turn, so they look to him to help them. Usually they ask why. Why did you do this to me? It is as if you believe in God but only think of him as a life

3. Luke 23:42.

preserver. You mess around and accidently fall off the boat. It is your fault. Then you come to your senses and ask God to save you. He was with you all along. You forget he is not a life preserver. He is the boat carrying you to your destination. How about we treat God with the respect he deserves? He has already provided us a safe passageway to salvation. He owes us nothing more. Just go get on the boat.

The second person realized there was so much more than this life. He believed in Jesus as king and asked for forgiveness. He feared God. He knew he had done wrong. He was repentant. He understood that it is by grace we receive anything.

Jesus told the second person, "Truly I tell you, today you will be with Me in Paradise."[4] Paradise? What is this paradise?

After Bev and I entered into our covenant relationship, I moved into the house she was currently renting. The place was okay but not where we wanted to stay. It did not take long and we decided to buy a new house. We wanted a place of our own. A place we could call home. We looked at several places and finally decided to buy a small house in a small town. It was not much but I was fond of that little home. Not because of its size or detail but because we shared good times there. It was exciting. We made plans for our future and just took time to love one another. We were very happy and it was like paradise to me.

Where do we live when we enter a covenant relationship with Jesus? I think of Earth like that rental house we had when we were first married. It is a fine place but it is not home. Jesus told this thief on that day, he would be with Jesus in paradise. Many times, we wrap ourselves around this idea of the location of this paradise. Some think it is here on Earth. Some think it is around us. Some think it is above us. Is that really the important part of that sentence? Paradise!

First, Merriam-Webster defines paradise as a place or state of bliss, felicity, or delight.[5] Secondly, the thief was told he would be with Jesus. Between those two items, I really do not care where it is located. Call it whatever you want. Place it wherever you want. I desire to be in this location. This is where I ultimately want to end up. In a state of bliss, next to Jesus, my Lord and Savior.

When we think about salvation, we think of it as a pulling away from something bad. Somebody pulling you out of the way of a speeding car or

4. Luke 23:43.

5. Merriam-Webster, "Paradise."

providing the Heimlich maneuver means saving you from death. Our focus is on removing the bad. We often do not think about salvation as being pushed into good. Oftentimes we think so hard about salvation from hell that we do not think about the greatness of our new home. When I married Bev, I did not think about her saving me from a life of solitude and loneliness. I thought about our life together and the home where we would live.

What is heaven going to be like? Jesus told his disciples he was going to prepare a place for them in his Father's house.[6] Isaiah tells us the blind will see, the deaf will hear, the lame will leap, and the mute will shout for joy. There will be singing, everlasting joy, and gladness, and sorrow will be gone.[7] In Revelation 21 John "saw the Holy City, the new Jerusalem, coming down out of heaven from God, prepared as a bride beautifully dressed for her husband."[8] That is a part of the inspiration behind this book. It continues, saying he will wipe away their tears, and there will be no more death or pain. Anytime I get down on the troubles this world has to offer, those words bring comfort and joy as I am reminded that heaven is my true home and I am currently just living in a foreign land.

Hebrews 12:22–23 states, "But you have come to Mount Zion, to the city of the living God, the heavenly Jerusalem. You have come to thousands upon thousands of angels in joyful assymbly, to the church of the firstborn, whose names are written in heaven. You have come to God, the Judge of all, to the spirits of the righteous made perfect." We are joint heirs with Christ, and as such, all heaven has to offer is ours.[9] Not just part of heaven, but all of heaven.

Therefore, in heaven we will finally see God and the angels, but who else will be there? Something else that happens when we get married is we get a new family. My wife came with a new dad, mom, sister, brother, cousins, uncles, aunts, etc. There will be new family members we have never known during our time on Earth. Who is the church of the firstborn, whose names are written in heaven? These are the people who have put their trust in Jesus Christ. There we will see family and friends who have put their faith in Christ and have gone on before us. Oh how wonderful that will be. It all just seems so perfect.

6. John 14:2–3.

7. Isa 35:5, 6, 10.

8. Rev 21:2–4.

9. Rom 8:17.

Notice, Jesus told the thief he would be with Jesus in paradise today. Not years from now. Not days from now. Today! This means the day we die. Our spirit is not going to be in the ground. We will be with Jesus immediately after death.

We learn how great the afterlife is going to be from Paul. Philippians 1:21 states, "For to me, to live is Christ and to die is gain." We have to understand from where Paul is coming. In 2 Corinthians 11:24–27 Paul states, "Five times I received from the Jews the forty lashes minus one. Three times I was beaten with rods, once I was pelted with stones, three times I was shipwrecked, I spent a night and a day in the open sea, I have been constantly on the move. I have been in danger from rivers, in danger from bandits, in danger from my fellow Jews, in danger from Gentiles; in danger in the city, in danger in the country, in danger at sea; and in danger from false believers. I have labored and toiled and have often gone without sleep; I have known hunger and thirst and have often gone without food; I have been cold and naked." Life was very tough for Paul, yet following Jesus was his greatest experience. Remember, Paul used to be a Pharisee, and as such, he had a good life. He knew he had to give that up. No matter his circumstances, he kept Jesus at the forefront of his mind. That is because he understood what was going to happen when we die. He understood there was a better place coming and that being in a relationship with Jesus was the way to attain this new home. He was willing to go through those tough times because he knew the ending would be paradise.

Have you ever taken a long trip? Maybe it was a business trip or vacation. I used to be a pilot for the airlines. I was gone on a trip for three or four days at a time. I could not wait to get home to be with my family. Even if it is a vacation, which people want to do to get away from their normal lives, they still eventually want to get back home. Second Corinthians 5:8 states, "We are confident, I say, and would prefer to be away from the body and at home with the Lord." Paul wanted to be present with Jesus in heaven.

When this physical body dies, the Christian's spirit goes to be with Jesus. Right now, I am on a business trip. The goal of my business is to share the good news with those who do not have it. There is a better day coming. There is a day coming when I will live in paradise. I long for that home.

Conclusion

READING THROUGH THE BOOK, were you able to determine why God gives us commands? Matthew 22 records a conversation about the greatest commandments. The Pharisees tried to test Jesus with his thoughts on the greatest commandment. Verses 37–40 state, "Jesus replied: 'Love the Lord your God with all your heart and with all your soul and with all your mind. This is the first and greatest commandment. And the second is like it: Love your neighbor as yourself. All the Law and the Prophets hang on these two commandments.'"[1]

First, notice the greatest commandment is to love God first. It is possible to love other humans and not love God, and this would be a mistake. Second, notice he said *all* the Law and Prophets hang on these two commandments. Everything God tells us to do falls into these two commandments. Why?

The Bible is filled with commandments from God. Take any commandment at random and break it down. For an example, I will choose, "Thou shall not steal."[2] Did God give us this command because he gets annoyed when we steal? I do not think so. We are not stealing from God. Does God love us less if we steal? I do not think so. As a father, I can tell you I would not love my daughter less if she stole, even if she stole from me. He still wants to be in a relationship with us.

Why give us the command? When we steal, we are not treating our neighbor properly. When we do not treat our neighbor properly, we damage a relationship between the two of us. God wants to have a family to love. He wants to be the loving Father. He wants his children to love each other. He wants to have a covenant relationship with us. If God wants us to be a loving family, we cannot go on damaging the relationships. We cannot

1. Matt 22:37–40.
2. Exod 20:15.

hate each other and take advantage of each other. Would that make sense? What if I went to my brother and said I was going to take advantage of him but he needed to love me anyway? That would be ridiculous. He gave us commands to keep the family intact.

"Thou shall not commit adultery."[3] Damage! "Thou shall not give false testimony against your neighbor."[4] Damage! "Thou shall not covet."[5] Damage! You can break down the commandments and see he gives them to us to help us keep good relationships. Try it for yourself. Pick out a commandment and try to figure out why he gave it to us. Did he give it because he wants a slave to serve him, or did he give it because it helps our relationships? It might mean our relationship with God or our relationship with each other. This is what Christianity is. It is a relationship, not a dictatorship.

He wants us to focus on go. He gave us the Great Commission so our spiritual family would be greater. He told us to go to church to help and show love to each other. He told us to communicate with him because communication helps the relationship. He told us to follow his ways because his ways are best, meaning we grow in the relationship. He gave us the rules in the Bible for our sakes. God is not a dictator, exasperating us like a slave. He wants us to be a family.

He wants us to enter a covenant with him and grow the family through adoption. He wants us to share a home together in the sky. He wants us to die to ourselves and change our identity. He offers the perfect situation. Why would we not want that?

We are so ready to accept the love of God, but we are less willing to allow ourselves to fall in love with God because falling in love is vulnerable. Falling in love is sacrificial. Falling in love means caring for somebody so much that you care less about yourself, for their sake. This is the very reason he gave us these commands. By doing them, and keeping our focus on the love, we grow stronger in our faith, and we mature in our relationships. Remember to keep the proper focus on this journey.

I have been married to my wife, Bev, now for over twenty-five years. I love my wife more now than I did when we first got married. We work at the relationship by attempting to please the other person. We have done so much for each other over the years. I became a living sacrifice for my wife. I am not a psychologist and I am not arrogant enough to think I have

3. Exod 20:14.

4. Exod 20:16.

5. Exod 20:17.

complete knowledge on keeping a relationship strong, but I feel if I am willing to die for her, and she is willing to die for me, the relationship has a greater chance of success. We wake up thinking love is a choice.

The same thing has happened with my relationship with Jesus Christ. I have worked on that relationship. Work comes through prayer, service, obedience, and learning. This work has helped me grow my relationship with him. If I am willing to die for God, the relationship has a greater chance at success. I love Jesus more now than I did when I first accepted him into my life.

One last thing about love. When I first asked Jesus into my life, it was because I did not want to go to hell someday. Different individuals come to Jesus for different reasons. As I matured, I wanted to stay in the relationship because Jesus loved me like no other person could. As I continued in this relationship, I found that I fell in love with Jesus because of who he is.

When I think about my relationship with Bev, we do not have to live in a big house and have fancy things. I will stand by her even if we end up homeless. After all, I took a vow for better or worse. With God, we may come to him for some other reason, like preventing hell or living in heaven someday. Those are selfish reasons. We are worried about what we get from the relationship. We need to grow and mature to the point that we want to please God instead of ourselves. I am not expecting to receive great materialistic earthly things for following Jesus. I just want to be with him. No matter where I go, I know I want to be in a relationship with Jesus because I love him. I will follow him wherever he goes and wherever he takes me.

This book considers the things I have learned in my walk with God. It is essentially the story of my salvation. I encourage you to look at your own lives and see if you can correlate them to living in a relationship with Jesus.

I was once asked to lead a group in a church lesson on short notice. I did not have a lesson prepared so I shared my salvation story and asked them to share their stories. That was one of the best nights of my life. Hearing how God has transformed hearts and lives is one of the greatest experiences I have ever encountered. We learned about each other and heard how great our God is. Imagine how great our heavenly family is going to be.

If you do nothing else, share your story. To keep your story to yourself denies Jesus a witness. The reason for writing this book is the hope that others will be able to find and have this great relationship. It has been the greatest thing for me, and I am positive it would be the best thing for you.

Bibliography

Aviation Instructor's Handbook: FAA-H-8083–9B. Federal Aviation Administration. Newcastle, WA: Aviation Supplies & Academics, 2008.

Braudrick, Jeremiah. *Removing the Dragon Skin: How C. S. Lewis Helped Me Get Over My Low Spiritual Self-Esteem and Fall Back in Love with God.* Eugene, OR: Wipf and Stock, 2019.

"CFI Checkride Coming Up with Rick Krietemeyer." JetCareers.com, July 28, 2012. https://jetcareers.com/forums/threads/cfi-checkride-coming-up-with-rick-krietemeyer.149072/.

Crosby, Donald A. *The Specter of the Absurd: Sources and Criticisms of Modern Nihilism.* New York: State University of New York Press, 1988.

Fiorillo, Steve. "How Much Does It Cost to Raise a Child in the U.S.?" *The Street,* December 19, 2018. https://www.thestreet.com/personal-finance/cost-to-raise-child-14814957.

Aviation Safety Network. "Flying Tiger Line 66—Aviation Accident Report." https://aviation-safety.net/database/record.php?id=19890219-0.

Hajek, Alan. "Pascal's Wager." *The Stanford Encyclopedia of Philosophy,* Summer 2018. https://plato.stanford.edu/entries/pascal-wager/.

Merriam-Webster. "Church." *Merriam-Webster,* 2020. https://www.merriam-webster.com/dictionary/church.

———. "Offense." *Merriam-Webster,* 2020. https://www.merriam-webster.com/dictionary/offense.

———. "Paradise." *Merriam-Webster,* 2020. https://www.merriam-webster.com/dictionary/paradise.

———. "Sacrifice." *Merriam-Webster,* 2020. https://www.merriam-webster.com/dictionary/sacrifice.

———. "Sin." *Merriam-Webster,* 2020. https://www.merriam-webster.com/dictionary/sin.

National Transportation Safety Board. "United Airlines 173—Aviation Accident Report AAR-79-77." April 6, 2000. https://www.ntsb.gov/Pages/Search.aspx?k=aar%2D79%2D07.

Sager, Lynn Marie. *A River Worth Riding: Fourteen Rules for Navigating Life.* Chula Vista, CA: Aventine, 2005.

Saint, Steve. *The End of the Spear: A True Story.* Carol Stream, IL: Tyndale, 2005.

Bibliography

Sherman, Alex. "Legal Gambling from Your Phone Could Be a $150 Billion Market, but Making It Happen Will Be Tough." *CNBC*, April 27, 2019. https://www.cnbc.com//2019/04/27/fanduel-draftkings-race-to-win-150-billion-sports-betting-market.html.

Strobel, Lee. *The Case for Christ: A Journalist's Personal Investigation of the Evidence for Jesus.* Grand Rapids: Zondervan, 1998.

Ziglar, Zig. *Confessions of a Happy Christian.* Gretna, LA: Pelican, 1993.

www.ingramcontent.com/pod-product-compliance
Lightning Source LLC
Chambersburg PA
CBHW071808090426
42737CB00012B/2000